BOB DYLAN THE LYRICS 1961—2020

"LOVE AND T.

"爱与窃"

鲍勃·迪伦诗歌集 1961—2020

VOL.09

[美]鲍勃·迪伦 著　李皖 译

中信出版集团 | 北京

被遗忘的时光
TIME OUT OF MIND

"爱与窃"
"LOVE AND THEFT"

摩登时代

MODERN TIMES

暴风雨
TEMPEST

TIME OUT OF MIND
被遗忘的时光

My heart's in the highlands at the break of day
Over the hills and far away
(I'm out there yet)
(There's a way to get there and I'll figure it out somehow
I'm there in my mind. That's good enough for now

自《红色天空下》之后，整整 7 年之久，迪伦没有发布原创专辑。

大约在 48 岁前后，也就是制作出版《哦，慈悲》的那一年，迪伦的创作心态发生了明显变化。灵感不常有，有了也不一定记下来，形成了词曲也不再有进录音室的冲动。

1991 年 4 月，他对来访者保罗·佐洛（Paul Zollo）说："曾经有个时期，歌曲会同时出现三四首，那些日子一去不复返了……偶尔，一首奇怪的歌会像一只斗牛犬站在门口，希望被写下来，但大多数都被我立刻拒绝了。你会疑心是否真的有人要听它。也许我写的歌够多了，让别人写吧。"

1996 年初，寒冬腊月中，迪伦在明尼苏达州的农场翻找出他五六年来写的歌（多数来自深夜，多数还只是歌词），他想到了曾一同制作《哦，慈悲》的丹尼尔·拉努瓦。二人相约在纽约见面，迪伦拿了一沓他写的歌词，念给拉努瓦听，问要不要录下来。拉努瓦觉得应该录："这些词很艰难，很深沉，很绝望，很强大……这就是我想要做的唱片。"

前所未有的，在正式录制之前，迪伦先用一些松散的、非正式的录音，制作这些歌曲的小样。1996 年秋天，这一阶段完成。

1997 年 1 月，二人开始正式录音，先在加州奥克斯纳德，后在迈阿密的标准录音工作室。迪伦不想离家太近，他想工作时与家保持距离。

拉努瓦组建了一支乐队。录音过程中，迪伦又另外选了些乐手，他想要现场演出的效果，他喜欢前科技时代的录音。"它们有自然的景深，而不是混合技术制造出的效果"，"那时技术没有超出艺术家的作为。现在最优先的是技术。这不是艺术家和艺术。"[1]

两组乐队竞争，两位制作人的观点也相左。极端时，录音室同有 3 位鼓手、5 位吉他手、2 位踏板吉他手，还有管风琴手、钢琴手……共 15 名乐手同时演奏。迪伦就靠在角落，被所有乐手包围，他们显得不知所措。刚开始场面一片混乱，这种情况持续了 1 个多小时，"后来有 5 到 8 分钟的时间，节奏非常清晰，所有人都找到了感觉。"[2]

全部歌曲都在 1997 年 1 月的两周内录完，大部分歌都是一次过。迪伦在距离麦克风 1 米的地方唱，没有戴耳机，只听屋里现场演奏的声音。然而，乐队的声音最后被过滤掉了，未用于唱片。迪伦的传记作者克林顿·海林说，

[1] Dylan, Bob (March 1999). "Guitar world interview" (Interview). Interviewed by Murray Engleheart.

[2] [法] 马戈汀，古斯登. 鲍勃·迪伦的歌：492 首歌背后的故事 [M]. 江岭，孙佳慧，郁梦非，等译. 郑州：河南大学出版社，2019.

拉努瓦制作了可能是迪伦经典中最做作的专辑，它听起来"就像拉努瓦的简历"。

唱片发行的最后一刻，迪伦决定雪藏，不发表。幸得索尼音乐娱乐公司总裁出面劝服，1997 年 9 月 30 日，《被遗忘的时光》以单张 CD 和双张黑胶两种形式，由哥伦比亚唱片公司发行，是为迪伦第 30 张录音室专辑。

这张专辑开启了迪伦的重返巅峰之路。在一些人心目中，它所带来的影响之大，近乎震动。埃尔维斯·科斯特洛（Elvis Costello）认为它是迪伦最好的专辑；《爱尔兰时报》2021 年的回顾文章直接把它排在迪伦全部 39 张录音室专辑的第一位。

《被遗忘的时光》的声音和气场，非常大气。迪伦此时 56 岁，却有一种行将就木的苍老感。以黑人老布鲁斯艺人的那种声音，他唱出了走在人生末路、走在天堂之途的感受。"在路上"一直是布鲁斯的母题，《被遗忘的时光》是另一种"在路上"。

《站在门口》《百万英里》《努力去天堂》《天还未暗》《等不及》都有站在门口或走在长路的感伤。天堂就在眼前，爱人遥不可及，不得其门而入。这是追寻了一生的结果，疲惫的身体和灵魂仍在路上，无悔而又无助。《相思病》《土路蓝调》《直到爱上你》《冰冷的镣铐》《让你感受我的爱》都表达了永久的爱，都是永恒的誓言；都是爱而不得却无怨无悔，依然是无条件的爱，依然是不灭的渴望。而所有这一切，都包裹在一种古老、梦幻、痛苦而又安详的气氛中。它们都是对死亡的沉思。

专辑以 16 分 31 秒的《高地》结束，灵感取自罗伯特·彭斯的《我的心在高地》。这首歌有着无比自由的叙事、联想和冥想，但显然，这"高地"不是苏格兰高地，而是天堂的隐喻。

LOVE SICK

I'm walking through streets that are dead
Walking, walking with you in my head
My feet are so tired, my brain is so wired
And the clouds are weeping

Did I hear someone tell a lie?
Did I hear someone's distant cry?
You thrilled me to my heart, then you ripped it all apart
You went through my pockets when I was sleeping

I'm sick of love . . . but I'm in the thick of it
This kind of love . . . I'm so sick of it

I see lovers in the meadow
I see silhouettes in the window
I watch them 'til they're gone and they leave me hanging on
To a shadow

I'm sick of love . . . I hear the clock tick
I'm sick of love . . . I'm love sick

Sometimes the silence can be like the thunder

相思病

我在业已死去的街道走着
走着，和我脑中的你一起走着
我的脚很累，头很迷糊
一片片云泪水低垂

我可听见有人在说谎？
我可听见远方谁在哭泣？
你让我的心战栗，然后把它撕碎
在我沉睡时，翻遍了我的衣袋

我厌恶爱情……却深陷其间
这一种爱情……太令我厌倦

我看到草地上的恋人
我看到窗户中的侧影
我望着，直到他们消失，直到他们
让我留存住，一个影子

我厌恶爱情……我听见时钟嘀嗒
我厌恶爱情……我得了相思病

有时沉默就像雷霆

Sometimes I feel like I'm being plowed under

Could you ever be true? I think of you

And I wonder

I'm sick of love . . . I wish I'd never met you

I'm sick of love . . . I'm trying to forget you

Just don't know what to do

I'd give anything to just be with you

有时我感到被翻到了最下一层
你能说实话吗？我想着你
我疑虑重重

我厌恶爱情……但愿从未相遇
我厌恶爱情……竭力将你忘记

只是不知该做什么
我愿付出一切，只要能与你一起

DIRT ROAD BLUES

Gon' walk down that dirt road, 'til someone lets me ride
Gon' walk down that dirt road, 'til someone lets me ride
If I can't find my baby, I'm gonna run away and hide

I been pacing around the room hoping maybe she'd come back
Pacing 'round the room hoping maybe she'd come back
Well, I been praying for salvation laying 'round in a one-room
    country shack

Gon' walk down that dirt road until my eyes begin to bleed
Gon' walk down that dirt road until my eyes begin to bleed
'Til there's nothing left to see, 'til the chains have been
    shattered and I've been freed

I been lookin' at my shadow, I been watching
    the colors up above
Lookin' at my shadow, watching the colors up above
Rolling through the rain and hail, looking for
    the sunny side of love

Gon' walk on down that dirt road 'til I'm right beside the sun
Gon' walk on down until I'm right beside the sun

土路蓝调

要沿着那土路走下去，直到有人载我一程
要沿着那土路走下去，直到有人载我一程
要是找不到我的宝贝，我将离去消失隐踪

我在屋里踱步，想她也许会回来
在屋里踱步，想她也许会回来
唉，游荡在一间房的村屋，我在
　　祈求救赎

要沿着那土路走下去，直到双眼流血
要沿着那土路走下去，直到双眼流血
直到什么都看不见，直到锁链粉碎
　　而我解脱

我低头看我的影子，我抬头望上面的
　　颜色
低头看我的影子，抬头望上面的颜色
翻滚着穿过雨幕冰雹，找寻爱情灿烂的
　　一角

要沿着那土路走下去，直到走到太阳边
要一直走下去啊，直到走到太阳边

I'm gonna have to put up a barrier to keep myself
  away from everyone

不得不竖起栅栏，将我与所有人

　　隔断

STANDING IN THE DOORWAY

I'm walking through the summer nights
Jukebox playing low
Yesterday everything was going too fast
Today, it's moving too slow
I got no place left to turn
I got nothing left to burn
Don't know if I saw you, if I would kiss you or kill you
It probably wouldn't matter to you anyhow
You left me standing in the doorway crying
I got nothing to go back to now

The light in this place is so bad
Making me sick in the head
All the laughter is just making me sad
The stars have turned cherry red
I'm strumming on my gay guitar
Smoking a cheap cigar
The ghost of our old love has not gone away
Don't look like it will anytime soon
You left me standing in the doorway crying

站在门口 [1]

我漫步走过夏夜
点唱机低低回旋
昨日一切太快
今天，进展太慢
再没有地方去
也没有什么还需要烧
不知道若见到你，我是会亲你还是把你杀了
对你而言可能都无所谓吧
你丢下我站在门口哭泣
我已身无一物还能回到此时

这地方光线太差
直让人头昏脑热
所有的笑都只是让我难过
星星变成了樱桃色
我拨弄着我华美的吉他
抽着廉价的雪茄
旧爱的幽灵尚在徘徊
看来也不急着离去
你丢下我站在门口哭泣

---

[1] 本篇由杨盈盈校译。

Under the midnight moon

Maybe they'll get me and maybe they won't
But not tonight and it won't be here
There are things I could say but I don't
I know the mercy of God must be near
I've been riding the midnight train
Got ice water in my veins
I would be crazy if I took you back
It would go up against every rule
You left me standing in the doorway crying
Suffering like a fool

When the last rays of daylight go down
Buddy, you'll roll no more
I can hear the church bells ringing in the yard
I wonder who they're ringing for
I know I can't win
But my heart just won't give in
Last night I danced with a stranger
But she just reminded me you were the one
You left me standing in the doorway crying
In the dark land of the sun

I'll eat when I'm hungry, drink when I'm dry
And live my life on the square

在这午夜月光里

也许他们会懂我也许不会
但不会是今夜，也不会是在这里
有些事我明白但不会说
我知道上帝的怜悯应该近了
我一直乘着这午夜列车
冰水流进了血管
如果把你带回来那我可真疯了
这有违所有的常理
你丢下我站在门口哭泣
遭罪得就像是一个傻瓜

当白昼最后几道光也落下
伙计，你将不再漂泊
我能听到院子里教堂的钟声
心想这是为谁在敲呢
我知道我赢不了
可我的心不会屈服
昨晚我和陌生女人跳舞
可她让我想到你才是我深爱的
你丢下我站在门口哭泣
在太阳的黑暗王国里

饿了就吃，渴了就喝
我本本分分过活

And even if the flesh falls off of my face

I know someone will be there to care

It always means so much

Even the softest touch

I see nothing to be gained by any explanation

There are no words that need to be said

You left me standing in the doorway crying

Blues wrapped around my head

哪怕皮肉从脸上凋落
我知道总会有人关心
即使最轻的触碰
也总是意味良多
我明白任何解释都没用
任何话都无需说出口
你丢下我站在门口哭泣
悲伤裹住了我的头

MILLION MILES

You took a part of me that I really miss
I keep asking myself how long it can go on like this
You told yourself a lie, that's all right mama I told myself one
   too
I'm tryin' to get closer but I'm still a million miles from you

You took the silver, you took the gold
You left me standing out in the cold
People asked about you, I didn't tell them everything I knew
Well, I'm tryin' to get closer but I'm still a million miles from
   you

I'm drifting in and out of dreamless sleep
Throwing all my memories in a ditch so deep
Did so many things I never did intend to do
Well, I'm tryin' to get closer but I'm still a million miles from
   you

I need your love so bad, turn your lamp down low
I need every bit of it for the places that I go
Sometimes I wonder just what it's all coming to
Well, I'm tryin' to get closer but I'm still a million miles from

百万英里

你带走了我的一部分，令我刻骨相思
我不断问自己这还要多久才会停止
你对自己撒了谎，没关系妈妈我也
　一样
我努力想靠近你，可依然距你一百万英里

你拿走了银，拿走了金
抛下我独立寒风里
人们问起你，我知道的我并没有都说
唉，我努力想靠近你，可依然距你一百万
　英里

我在无梦的梦中漂进漂出
将所有记忆抛入深深沟渠
做了许多从不想做的事
唉，我努力想靠近你，可依然距你一百万
　英里

我多渴望你的爱啊，请将你的灯调暗下去
为了我要去的地方，我需要它的一点一滴
有时我寻思着这将带来什么后果
唉，我努力想靠近你，可依然距你一百万

you

Well, I don't dare close my eyes and I don't dare wink
Maybe in the next life I'll be able to hear myself think
Feel like talking to somebody but I just don't know who
Well, I'm tryin' to get closer but I'm still a million miles from
     you

The last thing you said before you hit the street
"Gonna find me a janitor to sweep me off my feet"
I said, "That's all right, you do what you gotta do"
Well, I'm tryin' to get closer, I'm still a million miles from you

Rock me, pretty baby, rock me 'til everything gets real
Rock me for a little while, rock me 'til there's nothing left to
     feel
And I'll rock you too
I'm tryin' to get closer but I'm still a million miles from you

Well, there's voices in the night trying to be heard
I'm sitting here listening to every mind-polluting word
I know plenty of people who would put me up for a day or two
Yes, I'm tryin' to get closer but I'm still a million miles from you

英里

唉，我不敢闭目也不敢眨眼
也许下辈子我才能专注心念
仿佛就像对我从不认识的人在说话
唉，我努力想靠近你，可依然距你一百万
　　英里

你上路前说了最后一句
"我要去找个能把我迷倒的锅炉哥"
我说："好啊，去做你要做的"
唉，我努力想靠近你，可依然距你一百万英里

摇撼我吧可人儿，摇撼到让一切成真
摇撼我一小会儿，摇撼到完全失去
　　感觉
而我也会摇撼你
我努力想靠近你，可依然距你一百万英里

唉，这夜里有声音想被人听见
我坐这儿听着，那一个个玷染心灵的词
我认识许多人可以让我借宿一两天
是啊，我努力想靠近你，可依然距你一百万英里

TRYIN' TO GET TO HEAVEN

The air is getting hotter
There's a rumbling in the skies
I've been wading through the high muddy water
With the heat rising in my eyes
Every day your memory grows dimmer
It doesn't haunt me like it did before
I've been walking through the middle of nowhere
Trying to get to heaven before they close the door

When I was in Missouri
They would not let me be
I had to leave there in a hurry
I only saw what they let me see
You broke a heart that loved you
Now you can seal up the book and not write anymore
I've been walking that lonesome valley
Trying to get to heaven before they close the door

People on the platforms
Waiting for the trains
I can hear their hearts a-beatin'
Like pendulums swinging on chains

努力去天堂

空气越来越热
天上有隆隆巨响
我涉过深深泥水
眼中热力渐渐高涨
对你的记忆逐日模糊
不再像从前那样昼思夜想
一直走在乌有之乡的中途
努力去天堂，趁大门还没关上

以前在密苏里
他们不让我自由自在
我被迫匆忙离去
只眼见了他们让我看见的
你伤了一颗爱你的心
现在可以将书封起来，不用再写了
一直走在那孤独山谷中
努力去天堂，趁大门还没关上

月台上的人
都在等候列车
我能听见他们的心跳
就像钟摆在链条上摆荡

I tried to give you everything

That your heart was longing for

I'm just going down the road feeling bad

Trying to get to heaven before they close the door

I'm going down the river

Down to New Orleans

They tell me everything is gonna be all right

But I don't know what "all right" even means

I was riding in a buggy with Miss Mary-Jane

Miss Mary-Jane got a house in Baltimore

I been all around the world, boys

Now I'm trying to get to heaven before they close the door

Gonna sleep down in the parlor

And relive my dreams

I'll close my eyes and I wonder

If everything is as hollow as it seems

When you think that you've lost everything

You find out you can always lose a little more

I been to Sugar Town, I shook the sugar down

Now I'm trying to get to heaven before they close the door

我曾尽力给你一切
那些你内心渴望的
现在我难过地走在这条路上
努力去天堂，趁大门还没关上

我要顺流而下
到新奥尔良去
他们告诉我一切会好
可我不懂"好"是什么意思
我曾与玛丽·珍小姐同乘
玛丽·珍小姐在巴尔的摩有房子
我已经周游了世界，小子们
现在我努力去天堂，趁大门还没关上

要去客厅睡觉了
把那些梦再做一遍
我将闭上眼睛想
一切是否真的如所见般虚妄
当你以为已失去一切
总发现还可以再失去一些
我去过糖果城了，摇下了糖果
现在我努力去天堂，趁大门还没关上

'TIL I FELL IN LOVE WITH YOU

Well, my nerves are exploding and my body's tense
I feel like the whole world got me pinned up against the fence
I've been hit too hard, I've seen too much
Nothing can heal me now, but your touch
I don't know what I'm gonna do
I was all right 'til I fell in love with you

Well, my house is on fire, burning to the sky
I thought it would rain but the clouds passed by
Now I feel like I'm coming to the end of my way
But I know God is my shield and he won't lead me astray
Still I don't know what I'm gonna do
I was all right 'til I fell in love with you

Boys in the street beginning to play
Girls like birds flying away
When I'm gone you will remember my name
I'm gonna win my way to wealth and fame
I don't know what I'm gonna do
I was all right 'til I fell in love with you

Junk is piling up, taking up space

直到爱上你

哦，神经爆炸，身体紧绷
感觉整个世界将我钉在栅栏上
受打击太大，见过太多
再没什么能将我疗愈，除了你的抚摸
不知道该去干啥
一直都还好直到爱上你

哦，我的房子着火了，火焰冲上天空
我以为会下雨但云朵只是路过
感觉像是路到了头
但我明白上帝保佑他不会让我误入歧途
还是不知道该去干啥
一直都还好直到爱上你

街头小子们开始嬉闹
姑娘们喜欢飞走的鸟儿
我走了你会记住我名字
我一定要赢得那财富和名誉
不知道该去干啥
一直都还好直到爱上你

垃圾堆积，占满了空间

My eyes feel like they're falling off my face

Sweat falling down, I'm staring at the floor

I'm thinking about that girl who won't be back no more

I don't know what I'm gonna do

I was all right 'til I fell in love with you

Well, I'm tired of talking, I'm tired of trying to explain

My attempts to please you were all in vain

Tomorrow night before the sun goes down

If I'm still among the living, I'll be Dixie bound

I just don't know what I'm gonna do

I was all right 'til I fell in love with you

感觉眼睛要从脸上掉下来
汗水滴落，我瞪着地板
想着那再不会回来的女孩
不知道该去干啥
一直都还好直到爱上你

哦，我厌倦了说话，厌倦了解释
取悦你的努力全部白费
明天晚上太阳下山前
假如我还活着，我要到南方去
只是不知道该去干啥
一直都还好直到爱上你

NOT DARK YET

Shadows are falling and I've been here all day

It's too hot to sleep, time is running away

Feel like my soul has turned into steel

I've still got the scars that the sun didn't heal

There's not even room enough to be anywhere

It's not dark yet, but it's getting there

Well, my sense of humanity has gone down the drain

Behind every beautiful thing there's been some kind of pain

She wrote me a letter and she wrote it so kind

She put down in writing what was in her mind

I just don't see why I should even care

It's not dark yet, but it's getting there

Well, I've been to London and I've been to gay Paree

I've followed the river and I got to the sea

I've been down on the bottom of a world full of lies

I ain't looking for nothing in anyone's eyes

Sometimes my burden seems more than I can bear

It's not dark yet, but it's getting there

I was born here and I'll die here against my will

天还未暗

阴影重重落我已盘桓整日
天热睡不着，时光正在飞逝
感觉灵魂变成了钢铁
我依然带着伤，太阳也不能治愈
天下之大竟没有容身之所
天还未暗，但正在朝这儿赶

唉，我的人性已随下水道冲走
每一桩美事背后都藏着某种痛苦
她给我写了封信，信写得恳切
心里话她全都写了
我只是不明白我为什么还要在乎
天还未暗，但正在朝这儿赶

哦，我去过伦敦也去过乐都巴黎
跟随着河流我来到海上
我一直在充斥谎言的世界底部
不在别人的眼中找寻什么
有时候负担重得像是承不住
天还未暗，但正在朝这儿赶

我生于此也将死于此，尽管非我所愿

I know it looks like I'm moving, but I'm standing still

Every nerve in my body is so vacant and numb

I can't even remember what it was I came here

   to get away from

Don't even hear a murmur of a prayer

It's not dark yet, but it's getting there

我知道看似我在云游，其实一直呆立原地
全身每根神经都已失去知觉
我已记不起当初来此是为
　　逃离什么
甚至听不到祷告的低语
天还未暗，但正在朝这儿赶

COLD IRONS BOUND

I'm beginning to hear voices and there's no one around
Well, I'm all used up and the fields have turned brown
I went to church on Sunday and she passed by
My love for her is taking such a long time to die

I'm waist deep, waist deep in the mist
It's almost like, almost like I don't exist
I'm twenty miles out of town in cold irons bound

The walls of pride are high and wide
Can't see over to the other side
It's such a sad thing to see beauty decay
It's sadder still to feel your heart torn away

One look at you and I'm out of control
Like the universe has swallowed me whole
I'm twenty miles out of town in cold irons bound

There's too many people, too many to recall
I thought some of 'm were friends of mine,
    I was wrong about 'm all
Well, the road is rocky and the hillside's mud

冰冷的镣铐

开始我听见说话声，然而四下无人
唉，我精疲力竭，田野已是一片褐色
那个星期天我去教堂，她从身旁经过
对她的爱历经这么久，总算是解脱了

我在齐腰深、齐腰深的迷雾中
这情形就好像，就好像我不存在
我戴着冰冷的镣铐，在城外二十英里

自尊之墙高而且宽
看不到另一面
眼见着美丽枯萎，是多么伤心
更伤心的是感到你的心被生生撕去

看一眼你，我无法自持
就像宇宙将我整个吞噬
我戴着冰冷的镣铐，在城外二十英里

太多太多人，已无法记起
我以为其中有些是我朋友，
　　可我错了
唉，道路崎岖，山坡尽是泥泞

Up over my head nothing but clouds of blood

I found my world, found my world in you
But your love just hasn't proved true
I'm twenty miles out of town in cold irons bound
Twenty miles out of town in cold irons bound

Oh, the winds in Chicago have torn me to shreds
Reality has always had too many heads
Some things last longer than you think they will
There are some kind of things you can never kill

It's you and you only I been thinking about
But you can't see in and it's hard lookin' out
I'm twenty miles out of town in cold irons bound

Well the fat's in the fire and the water's in the tank
The whiskey's in the jar and the money's in the bank
I tried to love and protect you because I cared
I'm gonna remember forever the joy that we shared

Looking at you and I'm on my bended knee
You have no idea what you do to me
I'm twenty miles out of town in cold irons bound
Twenty miles out of town in cold irons bound

我的头顶只有一团血云

我找到了我的世界，在你里面找到我的世界
但你的爱没有被证实
我戴着冰冷的镣铐，在城外二十英里
戴着冰冷的镣铐，在城外二十英里

啊，芝加哥的风将我撕成碎片
现实总有着太多嘴脸
有些东西比你想象的命长
有些东西你无法让它消亡

我一直在想你，只有你
但是你看不到里面，也难注意到外面
我戴着冰冷的镣铐，在城外二十英里

哦肥油在火中，水在水箱里
威士忌在杯中，钱在银行里
我极力爱你护你，因为我在乎
我将永远记住，那一同走过的幸福

看着你，我单膝跪下
你如何待我，你一无所知
我戴着冰冷的镣铐，在城外二十英里
戴着冰冷的镣铐，在城外二十英里

MAKE YOU FEEL MY LOVE

When the rain is blowing in your face
And the whole world is on your case
I could offer you a warm embrace
To make you feel my love

When the evening shadows and the stars appear
And there is no one there to dry your tears
I could hold you for a million years
To make you feel my love

I know you haven't made your mind up yet
But I would never do you wrong
I've known it from the moment that we met
No doubt in my mind where you belong

I'd go hungry, I'd go black and blue
I'd go crawling down the avenue
There's nothing that I wouldn't do
To make you feel my love

The storms are raging on the rollin' sea
And on the highway of regret

让你感受我的爱

当雨水吹打着你的面容
而整个世界都在对你嘲讽
我会与你热情相拥
让你感受我的爱

当暮影重重星辰初现
没有人为你将泪擦干
我会拥抱着你一百万年
让你感受我的爱

我知道你的心还在动摇
然而我永不会将你错待
相遇的一刻我便知道
无疑我的心便是你之归属

我会忍饥挨饿，会领受累累伤疤
我会沿着大街爬
没什么是我不会做的
让你感受我的爱

风暴在翻滚的大海肆虐
在悔恨的高速公路肆虐

Put your hand in mine and come with me

I'll see that you don't get wet

I could make you happy, make your dreams come true

Nothing that I wouldn't do

Go to the ends of the earth for you

To make you feel my love

把手递给我跟我来
我确保你不会淋雨

我会叫你开心，让你美梦成真
没什么我不会做
为你走到世界的每个尽头
让你感受我的爱

CAN'T WAIT

I can't wait, wait for you to change your mind
It's late, I'm trying to walk the line
Well, it's way past midnight and there are people all around
Some on their way up, some on their way down
The air burns and I'm trying to think straight
And I don't know how much longer I can wait

I'm your man, I'm trying to recover the sweet love that we
   knew
You understand that my heart can't go on beating without you
Well, your loveliness has wounded me, I'm reeling from the
   blow
I wish I knew what it was keeps me loving you so
I'm breathing hard, standing at the gate
But I don't know how much longer I can wait

Skies are grey, I'm looking for anything that will bring a happy
   glow
Night or day, it doesn't matter where I go anymore, I just go
If I ever saw you coming I don't know what I would do
I'd like to think I could control myself, but it isn't true
That's how it is when things disintegrate

等不及

等不及，等不及你改变心意
太晚了，我还努力走在这路上
哦，午夜已过，到处是人
有的在上升，有的在下降
空气燃烧，我还在努力保持清醒
真不知道这样还能等多久

我是你的男人，试图寻回我们曾有过的
　浓情
你知道若没有你，我的心将无法继续跳动
哦，你的美让我受伤，我摇晃着躲避
　那重击
多想知道是什么让我仍如此爱你
呼吸沉重，我站在门口
可我不知道这样还能等多久

天空灰暗，我找寻着能带来幸福光晕的
　一切
无论昼夜，无所谓何方，我都会慨然前往
若真的见到你来，我会不知所措
我想我应该可以控制自己，但事实并非如此
事情崩溃时就是这样

And I don't know how much longer I can wait

I'm doomed to love you, I've been rolling through stormy
   weather
I'm thinking of you and all the places we could roam together

It's mighty funny, the end of time has just begun
Oh, honey, after all these years you're still the one
While I'm strolling through the lonely graveyard of my mind
I left my life with you somewhere back there along the line
I thought somehow that I would be spared this fate
But I don't know how much longer I can wait

真不知道这样还能等多久

爱你是我命中注定，一路翻滚着穿过
　风雨
我在想你，想所有我们能一起漫步之地

这实在是可笑，时间的终局才刚开始
啊，亲爱的，这么多年过去你仍是我的唯一
当我缓步走过我心灵寂寞的坟场
我把生命留给你了，在那回来的路上
我想这样或许能逃过此劫
可我不知道这样还能等多久

HIGHLANDS

Well my heart's in the Highlands, gentle and fair
Honeysuckle blooming in the wildwood air
Bluebells blazing where the Aberdeen waters flow
Well my heart's in the Highlands
I'm gonna go there when I feel good enough to go

Windows were shakin' all night in my dreams
Everything was exactly the way that it seems
Woke up this morning and I looked at the same old page
Same ol' rat race
Life in the same ol' cage

I don't want nothing from anyone, ain't that much to take
Wouldn't know the difference between a real blonde and a
   fake
Feel like a prisoner in a world of mystery
I wish someone would come
And push back the clock for me

高地 [1]

哦我的心在高地，明媚而和煦
金银花在野林空气中绽放
蓝铃在阿伯丁水流处闪光
哦我的心在高地
当我兴致高昂时，我将前往

睡梦中窗户整夜在晃
一切都正如看上去的那样
今早醒来，眼前还是此前景致
还是一样的你争我抢
生活还是在这只牢笼里

谁的东西我都不要，哪有那么多可拿的
真假金发女郎到底有何
　区别
感觉就像神秘世界的囚徒
我希望有人来
将时钟为我拨回去

---

[1]　这首歌词的副歌段落运用了苏格兰诗人罗伯特·彭斯《我的心在高地》的部分诗句。

Well my heart's in the Highlands wherever I roam

That's where I'll be when I get called home

The wind, it whispers to the buck-eyed trees in rhyme

Well my heart's in the Highlands

I can only get there one step at a time

I'm listening to Neil Young, I gotta turn up the sound

Someone's always yelling turn it down

Feel like I'm drifting

Drifting from scene to scene

I'm wondering what in the devil could it all possibly mean?

Insanity is smashing up against my soul

You can say I was on anything but a roll

If I had a conscience, well, I just might blow my top

What would I do with it anyway

Maybe take it to the pawn shop

My heart's in the Highlands at the break of dawn

By the beautiful lake of the Black Swan

Big white clouds like chariots that swing down low

Well my heart's in the Highlands

Only place left to go

哦我的心在高地，无论漂泊何处
只要回家的呼唤响起，我就要归去
风，对着鹿眼树悠扬低语
哦我的心在高地
只有一步一步，我才能回到那里

我在听尼尔·扬[1]，我必须开大声
老有人嚷嚷说"关小音量"
感觉我在漂浮
从一个场景漂向另一个
我寻思着这究竟是什么鬼意思？

疯狂正撞击着我的灵魂
你可以说我除了走运事事有份儿
如果我有良心，好吧，我就会冲冠一怒
到底我该如何处置这良心呢
也许是把它送进当铺

我的心在高地晨光初现
就在美丽的黑天鹅湖畔
大团白云如马车低低摆荡
哦我的心在高地
这剩下唯一可去的地方

---

[1] 尼尔·扬，与迪伦差不多同时期的加拿大著名歌手。

I'm in Boston town, in some restaurant
I got no idea what I want
Well, maybe I do but I'm just really not sure
Waitress comes over
Nobody in the place but me and her

It must be a holiday, there's nobody around
She studies me closely as I sit down
She got a pretty face and long white shiny legs
She says, "What'll it be?"
I say, "I don't know, you got any soft boiled eggs?"

She looks at me, says, "I'd bring you some
But we're out of 'm, you picked the wrong time to come"
Then she says, "I know you're an artist, draw a picture of me!"
I say, "I would if I could, but
I don't do sketches from memory"

"Well," she says, "I'm right here in front of you, or haven't you
    looked?"
I say, "All right, I know, but I don't have my drawing book!"
She gives me a napkin, she says, "You can do it on that"
I say, "Yes I could, but
I don't know where my pencil is at!"

She pulls one out from behind her ear

在波士顿城一家餐馆
我不知道自己要来点啥
好吧也许我知道，但是真不确定
女招待走了过来
整个地方就只有我和她

应该是假日，周围一个人都没有
当我坐下时，她仔细上下打量
她有漂亮的脸和又白又亮的长腿
她说："要点什么呢？"
我说："不知道，有溏心蛋吗？"

她看着我，说："我倒想给你来份儿
不过卖完了，你来得不是时候"
然后她说："我知道你是艺术家，给我画一张吧！"
我说："可能的话我会画，但是
我不凭记忆写生"

"呃？"她说，"我就在你面前，难道你
看不见？"
我说："好吧，我知道，可我没带画本"
她给我一张餐巾纸，说："可以画这上面"
我说："是的，可以，但是
不知道哪儿有铅笔！"

她从耳后抽出一支

She says, "All right now, go ahead, draw me, I'm standing
    right here"
I make a few lines and I show it for her to see
Well she takes the napkin and throws it back
And says, "That don't look a thing like me!"

I said, "Oh, kind Miss, it most certainly does"
She says, "You must be jokin'." I say, "I wish I was!"
Then she says, "You don't read women authors, do you?"
Least that's what I think I hear her say
"Well," I say, "how would you know and what would it matter
    anyway?"

"Well," she says, "you just don't seem like you do!"
I said, "You're way wrong"
She says, "Which ones have you read then?" I say, "I read
    Erica Jong!"
She goes away for a minute
And I slide up out of my chair
I step outside back to the busy street but nobody's going
    anywhere

Well my heart's in the Highlands with the horses and hounds

说："好了，来吧，画我，我就
　　站这儿"
我画了几笔，递给她看
哦她接过餐巾纸，又扔回来
一边说："看起来不像！"

我说："啊，善心的小姐，当然很像"
她说："你开玩笑吧。"我说："我倒希望是！"
她又说："你不读女作家，是吧？"
至少我以为我听她是这么说的
"好吧，"我说，"你怎么知道，这有什么
　　关系？"

"嗯，"她说，"你看起来不像读过！"
我说："你错了"
她说："那你读过谁？"我说："我读过
　　埃丽卡·容[1]！"
她走开了一会儿
我溜下座儿
回到外面，街上熙熙攘攘但人人
　　漫无方向

哦我的心在高地，跟马和猎犬一起

---

[1] 埃丽卡·容（1942—），美国女作家、诗人，其小说《怕飞》在第
　　二波女性主义运动中有重要地位。

Way up in the border country, far from the towns
With the twang of the arrow and a snap of the bow
My heart's in the Highlands
Can't see any other way to go

Every day is the same thing out the door
Feel further away than ever before
Some things in life, it gets too late to learn
Well, I'm lost somewhere
I must have made a few bad turns

I see people in the park forgetting their troubles and woes
They're drinking and dancing, wearing bright-colored clothes
All the young men with their young women looking so good
Well, I'd trade places with any of them
In a minute, if I could

I'm crossing the street to get away from a mangy dog
Talking to myself in a monologue
I think what I need might be a full-length leather coat
Somebody just asked me
If I registered to vote

The sun is beginning to shine on me
But it's not like the sun that used to be
The party's over and there's less and less to say

归向边境乡野，远离市镇
随着弓的一响和箭的一声
我的心在高地
看不到还有其他路可行

每天出门都是老一套
感觉比从前更远
人生有些事，要学已经太晚
唉，我在何处迷失
一定是错转了几个弯

我看见公园里的人忘记了烦恼和忧愁
他们饮酒跳舞，穿着鲜艳衣服
年轻男人和他们的年轻女人赏心悦目
哦，我愿与其中任一位调换位置
如果可以，请立刻

我横穿马路躲一条癞皮狗
自己跟自己唠叨
我想我也许需要一件长款皮衣
刚有人问我
有没有登记投票

太阳开始照在我身上
但不像是之前的那个太阳
聚会已经结束，越来越无话可谈

I got new eyes

Everything looks far away

Well, my heart's in the Highlands at the break of day

Over the hills and far away

There's a way to get there and I'll figure it out somehow

But I'm already there in my mind

And that's good enough for now

我有了新眼光
看什么都很远

哦，我的心在高地晨光初现
在山连山的那边，路途遥远
有一条路能到那儿，我会想方设法
而在心里我早已抵达
现在这样已经够好了

THINGS HAVE CHANGED

A worried man with a worried mind
No one in front of me and nothing behind
There's a woman on my lap and she's drinking champagne
Got white skin, blood in my eyes
I'm looking up into the sapphire-tinted skies
I'm well dressed, waiting on the last train

Standing on the gallows with my head in a noose
Any minute now I'm expecting all hell to break loose

People are crazy and times are strange
I'm locked in tight, I'm out of range
I used to care, but things have changed

This place ain't doing me any good
I'm in the wrong town, I should be in Hollywood
Just for a second there I thought I saw something move
Gonna take dancing lessons, do the jitterbug rag
Ain't no shortcuts, gonna dress in drag
Only a fool in here would think he's got anything to prove

事情变了

烦忧的人有颗烦忧的心
我身后无物，身前无人
有一个女人坐我腿上喝香槟
她皮肤白皙，我眼睛充血
我抬头看着蓝宝石的天野
衣冠楚楚，等待那最后一班列车

头戴套索站在绞架下
时刻准备着，一切陷落

人们全疯了，时代变得陌生
我被紧紧锁住，在这界程之外
我曾经很在乎，但现在事情变了

待在此地已一无是处
这是错误的城，我应该去好莱坞
有那么一瞬，我以为我看到事情有所松动
要去上舞蹈课，要学跳吉特巴 [1]
要穿上裙子逗乐，没什么捷径
只有傻瓜才以为他有什么非要证明

---

[1] 吉特巴，又称"水兵舞"，诞生于 20 世纪 20 年代，30 年代风行全球。

Lot of water under the bridge, lot of other stuff too
Don't get up gentlemen, I'm only passing through

People are crazy and times are strange
I'm locked in tight, I'm out of range
I used to care, but things have changed

I've been walking forty miles of bad road
If the Bible is right, the world will explode
I've been trying to get as far away from myself as I can
Some things are too hot to touch
The human mind can only stand so much
You can't win with a losing hand

Feel like falling in love with the first woman I meet
Putting her in a wheelbarrow and wheeling her down the street

People are crazy and times are strange
I'm locked in tight, I'm out of range
I used to care, but things have changed

I hurt easy, I just don't show it
You can hurt someone and not even know it
The next sixty seconds could be like an eternity
Gonna get low down, gonna fly high

桥下很多水，也有许多别的
不必起身先生们，我只是路过

人们全疯了，时代变得陌生
我被紧紧锁住，在这界程之外
我曾经很在乎，但现在事情变了

我已经走了四十英里烂路了
如果《圣经》是对的，那么世界将会爆炸
我一直在尽可能地远离自己
一些东西太热不能碰
人的头脑只能承受这么多
凭这副烂牌你不可能打赢

似乎是我爱上了我遇见的第一个女人
把她放在独轮车里，然后沿街推下去

人们全疯了，时代变得陌生
我被紧紧锁住，在这界程之外
我曾经很在乎，但现在事情变了

我容易受伤，只是不表露
你可能伤害了别人，自己却不知情
下一个六十秒可能就像永恒
做人要低调，做事要高调

All the truth in the world adds up to one big lie

I'm in love with a woman who don't even appeal to me

Mr. Jinx and Miss Lucy, they jumped in the lake

I'm not that eager to make a mistake

People are crazy and times are strange

I'm locked in tight, I'm out of range

I used to care, but things have changed

世界上所有的真相加起来是一个弥天大谎
我爱上一个女人，她甚至对我毫无吸引力

金克斯先生和露西小姐投了湖
我可没那么急于犯错

人们全疯了，时代变得陌生
我被紧紧锁住，在这界程之外
我曾经很在乎，但现在事情变了

RED RIVER SHORE

Some of us turn off the lights and we lay
Up in the moonlight shooting by
Some of us scare ourselves to death in the dark
To be where the angels fly
Pretty maids all in a row lined up
Outside my cabin door
I've never wanted any of 'em wanting me
'Cept the girl from the Red River shore

Well I sat by her side and for a while I tried
To make that girl my wife
She gave me her best advice when she said
Go home and lead a quiet life
Well I been to the East and I been to the West
And I been out where the black winds roar
Somehow, though, I never did get that far
With the girl from the Red River shore

Well I knew when I first laid eyes on her
I could never be free
One look at her and I knew right away
She should always be with me

红河岸

一部分人熄了灯，我们躺在
倾泻而下的月光中
一部分人在黑暗里，在这个天使飞翔的所在
把自己吓得要死
漂亮少女排成一排
在我的小木屋门外
我不希望她们中的任何一位要我
除了那个来自红河岸的女子

哦我坐在那女子身边，有一刻想要她成为
我的妻子
她给了我最好的建议，她说
回家去吧，过平静日子
嗯我去过东部，去过西部
也去过黑风呼啸之地
不过，不知为什么，我却从未走到那一步
与那个来自红河岸的女子

哦第一次看到她我就知道
我永远不可能有自由
一看到她，我立即就明白
她应该永远和我在一起

Well the dream dried up a long time ago

Don't know where it is anymore

True to life, true to me

Was the girl from the Red River shore

Well I'm wearing the cloak of misery

And I've tasted jilted love

And the frozen smile upon my face

Fits me like a glove

But I can't escape from the memory

Of the one that I'll always adore

All those nights when I lay in the arms

Of the girl from the Red River shore

Well we're livin' in the shadows of a fading past

Trapped in the fires of time

I tried not to ever hurt anybody

And to stay out of a life of crime

And when it's all been said and done

I never did know the score

One more day is another day away

From the girl from the Red River shore

Well I'm a stranger here in a strange land

But I know this is where I belong

I ramble and gamble for the one I love

唉这个梦久已干枯
不知道它现在何处
忠实于生活，忠实于我
就是那个来自红河岸的女子

哦我披着苦难斗篷
品尝过被遗弃的爱情
僵在我脸上的笑
与我相配得就像只手套
但我无法从记忆中
逃离我将永远爱慕的人
多少个夜晚我躺在她怀中
那个来自红河岸的女子

唉我们活在褪色往事的阴影中
受困于时光之火
我尽力不伤害谁
避免卷入犯罪生活
而当一切已成定局
我从来不知何来何去
多一天便是又去了一日
与那个来自红河岸的女子

唉此地是异乡而我是异客
但我知道这儿就是归宿
为了我爱的人我游荡、冒险

And the hills will give me a song
Though nothing looks familiar to me
I know I've stayed here before
Once a thousand nights ago
With the girl from the Red River shore

Well I went back to see about her once
Went back to straighten it out
Everybody that I talked to had seen us there
Said they didn't know who I was talkin' about
Well the sun went down a long time ago
And doesn't seem to shine anymore
I wish I could have spent every hour of my life
With the girl from the Red River shore

Now I heard of a guy who lived a long time ago
A man full of sorrow and strife
That if someone around him died and was dead
He knew how to bring him on back to life
Well I don't know what kind of language he used
Or if they do that kind of thing anymore
Sometimes I think nobody ever saw me here at all
'Cept the girl from the Red River shore

群山将赠我一曲
虽然这一切看上去都很陌生
但我知道我来过
在一千个夜晚之前
与那个来自红河岸的女子

哦有一次我回去找她
想把这事了结
问每一个见过我们的人
可他们就是不知我在说谁
哦太阳已经落下去很久
看来不会再升起
多希望我度过了一生中的每个时辰
与那个来自红河岸的女子

好吧我听说过一个活在很久前的人
一个充满了伤痛和矛盾的男子
如果有谁过世或久已亡故
他知道如何使他起死回生
唉不知道他用的是什么语言
不知道它们还起不起作用
有时候觉得这里就没人见过我
除了那个来自红河岸的女子

"LOVE AND THEFT"
"爱与窃"

The St. Regis
CLUB

Boys & Boys — Bo — Brethren Come Style CLUB

1c Every moment I'm not with you is a moment — despair —
 & but one girl in the world who you & I would compare
 Boy & Boy 5 Lu ~~baby~~ ~~everybody~~ ~~single~~ level g this 3 led me aro.

2. Priority the force / Spreading Revolution Abroad /
 Gonna establish my rule by civil war,
 Priority / turn/ if you got things I show you 2nd

3. Negotiate day Human bones on display —
 Gotta be quick on trigger — preserve a lot
 You hear how if people gonna help ya a lot — ⑤
    Bridge / Leh carve my initials on any mules behind
        The only thing he's able to see is one here & mind ←

9. Mix George — Dont ~~you~~ worry ~~you~~ — but you shut   He's in a rage —
    High brow Baby — Fo God's sake, can't you see   — stab stab stab on pistol
    How you funk it'd work if I did you still gonna say me on
    Dont believe / Dont believe him ... we gon = / Set our hearts together & make our plans to come
                                                / Still are gonna set our—

5. Miss Beth / Layin' on the couch —   Low down surrogat' leash
    He got his carbons drawn / Armies Alligon-d   And Mere stab ya when ya stood —
    With his poems to lose your mind
    Come down jingle man
        Bridge Iwy doing the hen percent boogie out on the north end of town
            Lets sit tight in the words you cant hear a sound

6 Prayer Gone Mad / Mann she feels bad   You promised me darlin'
    Smokestack erupting' shinin' like gold   The day that we met
    In gratitude just makes my blood run cold   that you always would luv me
                                                    Oh how you forget —
   feel
   realise the a Lefty it go ... 100 miles
   breaks   ~~all~~ I'm doing   for me, that's
            kill i said   too slow—

《被遗忘的时光》发行 4 年后，迪伦第 31 张录音室专辑《"爱与窃"》诞生。发行之日碰巧遇上"9·11"恐袭，但是劫难没能阻挡迪伦的成功，《"爱与窃"》成为恐怖袭击下"幸存"的热门专辑。

　　这是迪伦与他的"永不停止的巡演"伙伴们录制的第 1 张专辑。将一支与他整日厮磨的现场乐队带进录音室，用现场表演的方式录制新专辑，这个录音模式延续到他随后的 8 张录音室专辑中。

　　1999 年，迪伦制作了使他获得奥斯卡最佳电影原创歌曲的《事情变了》。不久后，他向巡演伙伴、吉他手兼多乐器演奏家拉里·坎贝尔（Larry Campbell）展示了新歌《可怜的孩子》的和弦进行。坎贝尔回忆："对迪伦的歌曲而言，这和弦进行相对复杂……这是对（接下来的专辑）材料的第一次暗示——从爵士乐时代汲取养分，为其添加民谣创作的灵感。"[1]

　　巡演的乐手们后来也都意识到了，在相当长的一段时

---

[1] Browne, David (September 11, 2016). "How Bob Dylan Made a Pre-Rock Masterpiece with 'Love and Theft'". *Rolling Stone*. Retrieved May 9, 2021.

间里，迪伦一点一滴地将《"爱与窃"》的乐思传递给他的团队。这是一张古老的唱片，来自真正早期的美国。没有人对美国音乐像迪伦了解得这么多。他花了一生的时间搜集和理解这些民间歌曲——一个永无尽头的资源宝库。鼓手戴维·肯珀（David Kemper）说："他（迪伦）总是想起我从未听说过的歌曲和艺术家。然后，当我们走进去录制《"爱与窃"》时，感觉就像是，噢上帝，他一直在教我们这种音乐——不是歌谱本上的歌曲，而是这些风格。作为一支乐队，我们熟悉其中每一个。这就是为什么我们可以每天录制完成一首歌……"

2001 年 5 月 18 至 26 日，除了《密西西比》，《"爱与窃"》的其余歌曲仅用 12 天即在纽约录制完成。迪伦放弃了编曲，现场录音仅给节奏、调号、风格、速度的提示，突然之间，乐队仿佛集体被民间的古老灵魂附体，这些歌曲成了。

专辑名出自音乐史学家埃里克·洛特（Eric Lott）1993年的著作《爱与窃：黑面人游艺表演与美国工人阶级》（*Love & Theft: Blackface Minstrelsy and the American Working Class*）。在 19 世纪末，白人艺人在脸上涂炭灰，模仿黑人歌舞，史称"黑面人游艺表演"。这是对黑人音乐的爱，也是窃；这里有摇滚乐深埋在密西西比三角洲最深的根脉，有美国南方的神话、秘谈和民间传说。

《可怜的孩子》听起来像是在 1920 年录制的。其他歌曲，也都听起来十分古早。迪伦的语气在谦逊与讽刺之间转换……要么搞笑，要么恐怖，要么兼而有之。一幅美国南方底层的全面肖像，在温柔又十足邪恶、凄怆又超冷幽默的调子中树立起来。

开场歌曲《大宝弟和大宝哥》，提到了新奥尔良狂欢节的游行，参与者戴着面具，尽管喝醉了，仍"决定一路这样走下去"。它像飓风一样席卷而来，讲述了一对可怜人的故事，以走向死亡结束——为一张充满了穷人、大兵、流浪汉、灾民、流氓、骗子、走私犯、赌徒和亡命之徒的专辑定了调子。其中的许多人都没有什么可失去的，有些人疯了，他们都是典型的美国人。

这些人是西部片和凯鲁亚克公路小说中令人一眼难忘的角色，这张专辑是 20 世纪 20 年代、30 年代和 40 年代的乡土美国。亡魂被唤醒了，已经消失的音乐精神重现了，历史上的古老声音和古旧风格——跳跃布鲁斯、慢速布鲁斯、乡巴佬摇滚、锡盘巷情歌、乡村西部摇摆……都变成了迪伦的声音。

它们是宿命的。它们是挽歌。它们深藏着世界末日的意象，有着又遥远又稀疏又无比情重的回响。

歌词中埋藏着民歌史的各种线索，有老民歌的各种关键词、妙语和意象。还有《漂浮者（过分的要求）》歌词，与日本作家佐贺纯一黑帮小说《浅草博徒一代》的英译本有多处相似，引起了"迪伦是否剽窃"的争议。

关于这方面，T. S. 艾略特早有名言："不成熟的诗人模仿，成熟的诗人偷窃。"罗伯特·克里斯戈则为迪伦辩护道："所有流行音乐都是爱与窃。迪伦 40 年的唱片中，其灵感来源曾激起大量的学术争论。然而哪一次都不像现在这样，如此热烈地拥抱了这个真理。"[1]

---

[1] Christgau, Robert (September 18, 2001). "Consumer Guide: Minstrels All". *The Village Voice*. Retrieved October 31, 2015.

TWEEDLE DEE & TWEEDLE DUM

Tweedle-dee Dum and Tweedle-dee Dee

They're throwing knives into the tree

Two big bags of dead man's bones

Got their noses to the grindstones

Living in the Land of Nod

Trustin' their fate to the hands of God

They pass by so silently

Tweedle-dee Dum and Tweedle-dee Dee

Well, they're going to the country, they're gonna retire

They're taking a street car named Desire

Looking in the window at the pecan pie

Lot of things they'd like they would never buy

Neither one gonna turn and run

They're making a voyage to the sun

"His Master's voice is calling me,"

大宝弟和大宝哥 [1]

大宝宝哥和大宝宝弟

他们掷飞刀去钉树

两大袋死人骨头

埋头苦干鼻子贴石头

他们住在挪得之地

将命运托付给上帝

他们过得无声无息

大宝宝哥和大宝宝弟

好吧，他们要去乡下，他们要退休

他们坐上了"欲望"号街车 [2]

望着窗里的山核桃派

许多东西喜欢却永远不买

哥俩谁都不会转身逃跑

这是朝着太阳的远行

"主人的声音在呼召我，"

---

[1] 歌名源自同名英语童谣："大宝哥和大宝弟 / 商量好要干一仗；/ 因大宝哥说大宝弟 / 弄坏了他的鼓拨浪。/ 这时飞来一只大老鸦，/ 黑得跟柏油桶一般；/ 两个英雄都吓怕，/ 浑忘了他们的争端。" 卡罗尔的《爱丽丝漫游奇境记》也写过这对互相争斗的兄弟。

[2] "欲望"号街车，美国剧作家田纳西·威廉斯有同名戏剧，曾拍成电影。

Says Tweedle-dee Dum to Tweedle-dee Dee

Tweedle-dee Dee and Tweedle-dee Dum
All that and more and then some
They walk among the stately trees
They know the secrets of the breeze
Tweedle-dee Dum says to Tweedle-dee Dee
"Your presence is obnoxious to me."
They're like babies sittin' on a woman's knee
Tweedle-dee Dum and Tweedle-dee Dee

Well, they're living in a happy harmony
Tweedle-dee Dum and Tweedle-dee Dee
They're one day older and a dollar short
They've got a parade permit and a police escort
Tweedle-dee Dee—he's on his hands and his knees
Saying, "Throw me somethin', Mister, please."
"What's good for you is good for me,"
Says Tweedle-dee Dum to Tweedle-dee Dee

Well a childish dream is a deathless need
And a noble truth is a sacred creed
They're lying low and they're makin' hay
They seem determined to go all the way
One is a lowdown, sorry old man
The other will stab you where you stand

大宝宝哥对大宝宝弟说

大宝宝弟和大宝宝哥

如此等等还有许多许多

他们走在雄伟的树林

他们知道微风的秘密

大宝宝哥对大宝宝弟说

"你的存在令我厌恶。"

像一个女人膝上的俩宝贝

大宝宝哥和大宝宝弟

好吧，他们过得和和气气

大宝宝哥和大宝宝弟

他们只老了一天只差了一元

有游行许可还有警察护送

大宝宝弟——他四脚着地

说："扔点啥给我吧，先生，求求你。"

"对你有好处的对我一样有好处，"

大宝宝哥对大宝宝弟说

哦童年的梦想是不死的渴望

有一条崇高真理是神圣的信仰

他们不吭气，他们逮住时机

他们似乎决定一路走下去

一个是下贱、可怜的老汉

另一个会在你的领地把你戳翻

"I've had too much of your company,"

Says Tweedle-dee Dum to Tweedle-dee Dee

"我已经受够了你的陪伴，"
大宝宝哥对大宝宝弟说

MISSISSIPPI

Every step of the way we walk the line
Your days are numbered, so are mine
Time is pilin' up, we struggle and we scrape
We're all boxed in, nowhere to escape
City's just a jungle, more games to play
Trapped in the heart of it, trying to get away
I was raised in the country, I been workin' in the town
I been in trouble ever since I set my suitcase down
Got nothing for you, I had nothing before
Don't even have anything for myself anymore
Sky full of fire, pain pourin' down
Nothing you can sell me, I'll see you around
All my powers of expression and thoughts so sublime
Could never do you justice in reason or rhyme
Only one thing I did wrong
Stayed in Mississippi a day too long

Well, the devil's in the alley, mule's in the stall
Say anything you wanna, I have heard it all

密西西比

我们这一路每一步都是定数
你的日子被数过，我的也是
时间堆起来，我们挣扎乱抓
被困在盒子中，想逃却没办法
城市就是丛林，有着太多游戏
在它中心陷入，再想方设法逃离
我在乡下长大，来到城里工作
一放下行李便麻烦不止
我没什么给你，以前的我一贫如洗
甚至都没啥留给自己
天空烈焰弥漫，痛苦兜头砸下
你没啥可卖给我，咱们回头见
我的表达能力和思维能力都棒极了
却没办法理性形象地说清你
只有一件事我铸成大错
就是在密西西比多待了一日

哦，魔鬼进了巷子，骡子进了马棚 [1]
说你想说的吧，我洗耳恭听

---

[1] 被别家的骡子进了自家的厩舍，在美国俚语中是"被戴绿帽"的
意思。

I was thinkin' about the things that Rosie said

I was dreaming I was sleeping in Rosie's bed

Walking through the leaves, falling from the trees

Feeling like a stranger nobody sees

So many things that we never will undo

I know you're sorry, I'm sorry too

Some people will offer you their hand and some won't

Last night I knew you, tonight I don't

I need somethin' strong to distract my mind

I'm gonna look at you 'til my eyes go blind

Well I got here following the southern star

I crossed that river just to be where you are

Only one thing I did wrong

Stayed in Mississippi a day too long

Well my ship's been split to splinters and it's sinking fast

I'm drownin' in the poison, got no future, got no past

But my heart is not weary, it's light and it's free

I've got nothin' but affection for all those who've sailed with me

Everybody movin' if they ain't already there

Everybody got to move somewhere

Stick with me baby, stick with me anyhow

Things should start to get interesting right about now

My clothes are wet, tight on my skin

我在想罗希 [1] 讲的事儿

我梦见我睡在罗希枕边儿

举步穿过纷纷落叶

感觉就像没人看见的异乡客

太多事永远无法解扣

我知道你歉疚，我也歉疚

有人会向你施援手，有人不会

昨晚我还了解你，今晚就一头雾水

我需要强烈的事分分心

要一直望着你，直望到双目失明

哦我追随南天星来到此地

渡过那条河只为来看你

只有一件事我铸成大错

就是在密西西比多待了一日

哦船成了碎片，转眼沉底

致命的幻觉淹没我，没有未来，没有过去

可我的心不倦怠，它轻盈，它自在

什么都没有了，只剩下我对同渡人的爱

每个人都在动，如果他还身在半途

每个人都必须移往他处

贴紧我宝贝，无论如何贴紧

事情开始变得有意思了

我的衣服湿透了，紧贴着皮肤

---

[1] 罗希，美国传统民谣中常出现，是黑人囚歌中的理想女性形象。

Not as tight as the corner that I painted myself in

I know that fortune is waitin' to be kind

So give me your hand and say you'll be mine

Well, the emptiness is endless, cold as the clay

You can always come back, but you can't come back all the

way

Only one thing I did wrong

Stayed in Mississippi a day too long

却并没有紧得像我把自己逼到绝处
我知道命运在等待仁慈
所以把手给我，说你以后就是我的
哦，空虚无边无际，冷得像片黏土
你可以随时回来，但不可能走
　　原路
只有一件事我铸成大错
就是在密西西比多待了一日

SUMMER DAYS

Summer days, summer nights are gone
Summer days and the summer nights are gone
I know a place where there's still somethin' going on

I got a house on a hill, I got hogs all out in the mud
I got a house on a hill, I got hogs out lying in the mud
Got a long haired woman, she got royal Indian blood

Everybody get ready—lift up your glasses and sing
Everybody get ready to lift up your glasses and sing
Well, I'm standin' on the table, I'm proposing a toast
    to the King

Well, I'm drivin' in the flats in a Cadillac car
The girls all say, "You're a worn out star."
My pockets are loaded and I'm spending every dime
How can you say you love someone else when you know it's
    me all the time?

Well, the fog's so thick you can't spy the land
The fog is so thick that you can't even spy the land
What good are you anyway, if you can't stand up to some old

夏日

夏日、夏夜已逝
夏日和那些夏夜已逝
我知道有个地方故事仍在继续

我在山上有座房，我在泥巴里养了猪
我在山上有座房，我在泥巴里养了些猪
讨了个长发女人，她是印第安王室的后裔

大家准备好——举杯开始唱
大家准备好举杯开始唱
哦，我站上桌子，我提议干杯
   敬祝国王

哦，我在公寓里开凯迪拉克
姑娘们都说："你是过气明星了。"
我的口袋满了，然后我花掉每个钢镚儿
你明晓得从头到尾都是我，怎能说
   你爱别人？

哦，大雾太浓你看不见陆地
大雾太浓你根本看不见陆地
如果连个老商贩都忍不了，你还

business man?

Wedding bells ringin', the choir is beginning to sing
Yes, the wedding bells are ringing and the choir is beginning
   to sing
What looks good in the day, at night is another thing

She's looking into my eyes, she's holding my hand
She's looking into my eyes, she's holding my hand
She says, "You can't repeat the past." I say, "You can't? What do
   you mean, you can't? Of course you can."

Where do you come from? Where do you go?
Sorry that's nothin' you would need to know
Well, my back has been to the wall for so long, it seems like
   it's stuck
Why don't you break my heart one more time just for good luck

I got eight carburetors, boys, I'm using 'em all
Well, I got eight carburetors and boys, I'm using 'em all
I'm short on gas, my motor's starting to stall

My dogs are barking, there must be someone around
My dogs are barking, there must be someone around
I got my hammer ringin', pretty baby, but the nails
   ain't goin' down

有什么用？

婚礼钟声响了，唱诗班开始唱
是的，婚礼钟声敲响了唱诗班
　　开始唱
白天看着漂亮，晚上是另一番模样

她望着我的眼，她握着我的手
她望着我的眼，她握着我的手
她说："你不能重复过去。"我说："你不能？
　　你什么意思，你不能？你当然可以。"

你从哪儿来？你到哪儿去？
抱歉，这不是你必须知道的
哦，我背靠墙太久，好像
　　粘住了
何不让我再心碎一次只为了祝你好运

我有八个化油器，小子们，我全打开
哦，我有八个化油器小子们，我全打开
我没油了，我的发动机就要停摆

我的狗在叫，一准儿有人在附近
我的狗在叫，一准儿有人在附近
我把锤子抡得呜呜响，美人儿，但钉子
　　就是纹丝不动

You got something to say, speak or hold your peace

Well, you got something to say, speak now or hold your peace

If it's information you want you can go get it from the police

Politician got on his jogging shoes

He must be running for office, got no time to lose

You been suckin' the blood out of the genius of generosity

You been rolling your eyes—you been teasing me

Standing by God's river, my soul is beginnin' to shake

Standing by God's river, my soul is beginnin' to shake

I'm countin' on you love, to give me a break

Well, I'm leaving in the morning as soon as the dark clouds lift

Yes, I'm leaving in the morning just as soon as the dark clouds
lift

Gonna break in the roof—set fire to the place as a parting gift

Summer days, summer nights are gone

Summer days, summer nights are gone

I know a place where there's still somethin' going on

你有话要讲，讲吧，否则请安静
哦，你有话要讲，现在讲吧，否则请安静
如果你想要听消息你可以到警察局打听

政客穿上了慢跑鞋
他一准儿在竞选，一刻都不耽误
你从慷慨的天才身上吸足了血
你转着眼珠子——你一直在取笑我

站在神的河边，我的灵魂开始战栗
站在神的河边，我的灵魂开始战栗
我就靠你了爱人，让我喘口气

哦，早上乌云一散我就离去
是的，早上乌云一散我就
　　离去
真想发飙———把火烧了这儿就当是分手礼

夏日、夏夜已逝
夏日、夏夜已逝
我知道有个地方故事仍在继续

BYE AND BYE

Bye and bye, I'm breathin' a lover's sigh
I'm sittin' on my watch so I can be on time
I'm singin' love's praises with sugar-coated rhyme
Bye and bye, on you I'm casting my eye

I'm paintin' the town—swinging my partner around
I know who I can depend on, I know who to trust
I'm watchin' the roads, I'm studying the dust
I'm paintin' the town making my last go-round

Well, I'm slippin' and slidin', walkin' on briars
To get to the one that my heart desires

I'm rollin' slow—I'm doing all I know
I'm tellin' myself I found true happiness
That I've still got a dream that hasn't been repossessed
I'm rollin' slow, goin' where the wild red roses grow

Well the future for me is already a thing of the past
You were my first love and you will be my last

Papa gone mad, mama, she's feeling sad

不久的将来

不久的将来，我将发出恋人的叹息
我将坐在手表上这样我就能准时
我将用穿糖衣的韵唱出爱的颂词
不久的将来，我将眼光投向你

我将满城狂欢——甩着我的舞伴团团转
我知道谁可相依，知道谁堪信任
我会看着路，我将研究飞尘
我将满城狂欢走好我的最后一圈

哦，穿过荆棘，我踉踉跄跄
奔向那唯一她是我心尖上的渴望

我将慢慢摇——做尽所有我知道的
我将对自己说我找到了真正的幸福
那是我尚未被上天收回的梦
我将慢慢摇，摇向红色野玫瑰生长的乐土

哦未来对我来说已经成为过去
你是我的最初，也将是我最后的爱侣

爸爸疯了，妈妈，她很伤心

I'll establish my rule through civil war

Bring it on up from the ocean's floor

I'll take you higher just so you can see the fire

我将通过内战建立起我的统治
从大洋底部一直往上升
我将带你飞更高由此看到那火焰腾腾

LONESOME DAY BLUES

Well, today has been a sad ol' lonesome day
Yeah, today has been a sad ol' lonesome day
I'm just sittin' here thinking
With my mind a million miles away

Well, they're doing the double shuffle, throwin' sand
    on the floor
They're doing the double shuffle, they're throwin' sand
    on the floor
When I left my long-time darlin'
She was standing in the door

Well, my pa he died and left me, my brother got killed
    in the war
Well, my pa he died and left me, my brother got killed
    in the war
My sister, she ran off and got married
Never was heard of any more

Samantha Brown lived in my house for about

寂寞日蓝调

唉，今天成了难过的寂寞日
是啊，今天成了难过的寂寞日
我就坐这儿傻想
心思飞到了百万英里外

唉，他们跳着双人曳步，把沙子
　　甩向地板
他们跳着双人曳步，他们把沙子
　　甩向地板
我离开了我的老情人
当时她就站在门前

唉，我爸死了抛下我，我兄弟
　　在战争中送了命
唉，我爸死了抛下我，我兄弟
　　在战争中送了命
我姐姐，她私奔嫁人了
再没有任何音讯

萨曼莎·布朗 [1] 在我家住了差不多

---

[1] 萨曼莎·布朗（1970— ），美国电视主持人，主持旅游节目。

four or five months
Samantha Brown lived in my house for about
    four or five months
Don't know how it looked to other people
I never slept with her even once

The road's washed out—weather not fit for man or beast
Yeah, the road's washed out—weather not fit for man or beast
Funny how the things you have the hardest time parting with
Are the things you need the least

I'm forty miles from the mill—I'm droppin' it into overdrive
I'm forty miles from the mill—I'm droppin' it into overdrive
Got my dial set on the radio
I'm telling myself I'm still alive

I see your lover-man comin'—comin' 'cross the barren field
I see your lover-man comin'—comin' 'cross the barren field
He's not a gentleman at all—he's rotten to the core
He's a coward and he steals

Well my captain he's decorated—he's well schooled
    and he's skilled
My captain, he's decorated—he's well schooled and he's skilled
He's not sentimental—don't bother him at all
How many of his pals have been killed

四五个月
萨曼莎·布朗在我家住了差不多
　四五个月
不知道别人会怎么看
反正我一次也没跟她睡过

道路被冲毁了——这天气不适合人和兽
是啊，道路被冲毁了——这天气不适合人和兽
好笑啊你觉得最难舍的东西
就是你最不需要的

我离磨坊有四十英里——我推到超速挡
我离磨坊有四十英里——我推到超速挡
转动着收音机旋钮
我告诉自己还活在世上

我看见你的情人来了——他穿过这片不毛之地
我看见你的情人来了——他穿过这片不毛之地
他根本不是什么绅士——他烂到心儿了
他是个懦夫他还偷东西

哦我的头儿他得了勋章——他受过好教育
　他很懂行
我的头儿，他得了勋章——他受过好教育他很懂行
他从不感情用事——千万别打扰他
他有多少好兄弟被送了葬

Last night the wind was whisperin', I was trying to make out
  what it was
Last night the wind was whisperin' somethin'—I was trying to
  make out what it was
I tell myself something's comin'
But it never does

I'm gonna spare the defeated—I'm gonna speak to the crowd
I'm gonna spare the defeated, boys, I'm going to speak
  to the crowd
I am goin' to teach peace to the conquered
I'm gonna tame the proud

Well the leaves are rustlin' in the wood—things are fallin' off
  of the shelf
Leaves are rustlin' in the wood—things are fallin' off the shelf
You gonna need my help, sweetheart
You can't make love all by yourself

昨夜风低语，我使劲儿想听
　清楚
昨夜风低语着什么——我使劲儿
　想听清楚
我心说有事发生
但实际上百事皆无

我要饶了战败者——我要对民众讲话
我要饶了战败者，小子们，我将
　对民众讲话
我要向被征服者传授和平
我要让骄傲的人听话

哦树叶在林中沙沙响——物品从架子上
　跌落
树叶在林中沙沙响——物品从架子上跌落
你会需要我的帮助，心肝儿
做爱你一个人没法做

FLOATER
(TOO MUCH TO ASK)

Down over the window

Comes the dazzling sunlit rays

Through the back alleys—through the blinds

Another one of them endless days

Honey bees are buzzin'

Leaves begin to stir

I'm in love with my second cousin

I tell myself I could be happy forever with her

I keep listenin' for footsteps

But I ain't hearing any

From the boat I fish for bullheads

I catch a lot, sometimes too many

A summer breeze is blowing

A squall is settin' in

Sometimes it's just plain stupid

To get into any kind of wind

The old men 'round here, sometimes they get

漂浮者
（过分的要求）[1]

从窗户上下来

是那让人眼花的太阳光线

穿过了背街小巷——穿过了百叶窗

永无终点的日子里的又一天

蜜蜂嗡嗡嗡

树叶开始搅动

我爱上了远房表妹

心说跟她在一起永远都开心

我一直在听脚步声

但没听见什么

我从船上钓鲇鱼

钓了好多，有时候太多

一缕夏日微风吹过

一场暴风正在生成

有时候真够蠢的

竟然会陷入一阵风中

这儿的老年人，有时候会

---

[1]　这首歌多处引用了日本当代作家佐贺纯一的黑帮小说《浅草博徒一代》英译本中的句子。

On bad terms with the younger men
But old, young, age don't carry weight
It doesn't matter in the end
One of the boss' hangers-on
Comes to call at times you least expect
Try to bully ya—strong arm you—inspire you with fear
It has the opposite effect
There's a new grove of trees on the outskirts of town
The old one is long gone
Timber two-foot six across
Burns with the bark still on
They say times are hard, if you don't believe it
You can just follow your nose
It don't bother me—times are hard everywhere
We'll just have to see how it goes

My old man, he's like some feudal lord
Got more lives than a cat
Never seen him quarrel with my mother even once
Things come alive or they fall flat
You can smell the pinewood burnin'
You can hear the school bell ring
Gotta get up near the teacher if you can
If you wanna learn anything
Romeo, he said to Juliet, "You got a poor complexion.
It doesn't give your appearance a very youthful touch!"

和年轻人闹不和

但是老啊小啊，年纪不重要

到头来都不算什么

那老板的一个跟班儿

总是在你最意想不到时来访

想欺负你——施以高压——唤起你的恐惧

却适得其反

市郊有片新树林

老的那片久已不存

直径两英尺六的木材

连皮一直烧到如今

他们说时世艰难，你若是不信

跟着你的鼻子走一下便知

这不会影响我——哪里都是时世艰难

我们只需要看看它是怎么回事

我家的老爷子，就像是封建领主

一副不死身比猫都多命

从未见他跟我妈吵过一次

无论日子红火还是陷入困境

你能闻到松木烧燃

你能听到校园铃声

尽量接近老师如果有条件

如果你真想学点东西

罗密欧对朱丽叶说："你脸色很差

一点都不显年轻！"

Juliet said back to Romeo, "Why don't you just shove off
If it bothers you so much."
They all got out of here any way they could
The cold rain can give you the shivers
They went down the Ohio, the Cumberland, the Tennessee
All the rest of them rebel rivers

If you ever try to interfere with me or cross my path again
You do so at the peril of your own life
I'm not quite as cool or forgiving as I sound
I've seen enough heartaches and strife
My grandfather was a duck trapper
He could do it with just dragnets and ropes
My grandmother could sew new dresses out of old cloth
I don't know if they had any dreams or hopes
I had 'em once though, I suppose, to go along
With all the ring dancin' Christmas carols on all of the
    Christmas Eves
I left all my dreams and hopes
Buried under tobacco leaves
It's not always easy kicking someone out
Gotta wait a while—it can be an unpleasant task
Sometimes somebody wants you to give something up
And tears or not, it's too much to ask

朱丽叶回敬罗密欧："何不走远点儿
如果这让你这么烦心。"
他们都想方设法离开了这儿
那冷雨会让你一阵阵战栗
他们去了俄亥俄、坎伯兰、田纳西
其余的都在叛乱流域 [1]

如果你还想干涉或再挡我的道
这只会危及你自己的性命
我可不像表面上那么冷静仁慈
我看过够多的伤痛和纷争
我祖父是个捕野鸭的
做这事他只需要绳和网
我祖母会用旧布制新衣
我不知道他们有没有梦或希望
我倒是有过，我觉得，那就是
在每一个平安夜，在圣诞歌中跟人
　　跳舞转圈
这所有的梦和希望
我把它们埋在了烟草下面
踢开一个人并不总是容易
要等一会儿——这会是个不愉快的活儿
有时候有人要你放弃一些什么
不管泪流与否，这都是过分的要求

---

[1] 美国南北战争时期，美利坚合众国（北军）控制了大部分南方水域，
　　美利坚联盟国（南军）残部据守密西西比河上游，泛称"叛乱流域"。

HIGH WATER
(FOR CHARLEY PATTON)

High water risin'—risin' night and day
All the gold and silver are being stolen away
Big Joe Turner lookin' east and west
From the dark room of his mind
He made it to Kansas City
Twelfth Street and Vine
Nothing standing there
High water everywhere

High water risin', the shacks are slidin' down
Folks lose their possessions—folks are leaving town
Bertha Mason shook it—broke it
Then she hung it on a wall
Says, "You're dancin' with whom they tell you to
Or you don't dance at all."
It's tough out there

洪水
（献给查理·帕顿 [1]）

洪水上涨——日夜上涨

金银财宝被偷个精光

"大块头"乔·特纳 [2] 东瞧西看

从他心里的黑屋

可算是到了堪萨斯

第十二街和万恩路

可那里什么都站不住

到处洪水滔天

洪水上涨，棚屋被夷平

人们失去财产——人们离开城镇

伯莎·梅森 [3] 又摇——又撞

接着把它吊上墙

说："你要跟他们指定的人跳舞

否则就不要跳了。"

外面真是艰难

---

[1]　查理·帕顿（1891—1934），美国蓝调歌手，有"三角洲蓝调之父"之称，其歌曲《到处洪水滔天》讲述 1927 年密西西比河洪水的灾难。

[2]　大块头乔·特纳（1911—1985），美国蓝调歌手，绰号"蓝调老大"。

[3]　伯莎·梅森，小说《简·爱》中男主角的疯妻，查理·帕顿的妻子也叫伯莎。

High water everywhere

I got a cravin' love for blazing speed
Got a hopped up Mustang Ford
Jump into the wagon, love, throw your panties overboard
I can write you poems, make a strong man lose his mind
I'm no pig without a wig
I hope you treat me kind
Things are breakin' up out there
High water everywhere

High water risin', six inches 'bove my head
Coffins droppin' in the street
Like balloons made out of lead
Water pourin' into Vicksburg, don't know what I'm going to do
"Don't reach out for me," she said
"Can't you see I'm drownin' too?"
It's rough out there
High water everywhere

到处洪水滔天

我渴望风驰电掣的速度
我有辆改装的"野马福特"[1]
快上车，亲爱的，把裤衩甩车外去
我会给你写诗，叫硬汉干瞪眼
我可不是没假发的猪[2]
希望你对我好一点
一切都在崩盘
到处洪水滔天

洪水上涨，高过我头顶六寸
棺材扔在街上
像是一个个铅气球[3]
水涌入维克斯堡[4]，我不知道怎么办
"别伸手拽我，"她说
"没看到我也快淹死了吗？"
外面真是艰难
到处洪水滔天

---

[1] "野马福特"，美国福特生产的一种跑车。
[2] 没假发的猪，典出英国诗人克里斯蒂娜·罗塞蒂的诗《如果猪戴上假发》。
[3] 铅气球，英语中比喻无用、不被接受、头脑昏沉等。
[4] 维克斯堡，美国密西西比州城市，1927 年洪灾时收容了大批难民。

Well, George Lewis told the Englishman, the Italian and the Jew

"Don't open up your mind, boys,

To every conceivable point of view."

They got Charles Darwin trapped out there on Highway Five

Judge says to the High Sheriff

"I want him dead or alive

Either one, I don't care."

High water everywhere

The Cuckoo is a pretty bird, she warbles as she flies

I'm preachin' the word of God

I'm puttin' out your eyes

I asked Fat Nancy for something to eat, she said, "Take it off the
    shelf—

As great as you are, man,

You'll never be greater than yourself."

I told her I didn't really care

High water everywhere

I'm gettin' up in the morning—I believe I'll dust my broom

Keeping away from the women

I'm givin' 'em lots of room

哦，乔治·刘易斯[1]告诫英人、意人和犹太人

"孩子们，别对每一个可能的观点

都敞开心扉。"

他们把查尔斯·达尔文困在了五号公路

法官对警长说

"给我捉住他，是死是活

随便怎样，我不管。"

到处洪水滔天

杜鹃是只漂亮鸟，她边飞边鸣啭

"我在传神的福音

我要挖出你的眼"

我向胖南希要吃的，她说："自己

　　去架上拿——

你都这么大了，小伙子，

你永远不会比你本人更伟大。"

我告诉她我真的不在乎

到处洪水滔天

我早上起床——我相信我会弄干净我的扫帚

远离那些女人

保持足够距离

---

[1] 乔治·亨利·刘易斯（1817—1878），英国哲学家，达尔文的支持者。

Thunder rolling over Clarksdale, everything is looking blue

I just can't be happy, love

Unless you're happy too

It's bad out there

High water everywhere

雷霆滚过克拉克斯代尔 [1]，一切呈蓝色

我就是乐不起来，亲爱的

除非你也快乐

外面真是糟糕

到处洪水滔天

---

[1] 克拉克斯代尔，美国密西西比州城市，蓝调发祥地之一。

MOONLIGHT

The seasons they are turnin'
And my sad heart is yearnin'
To hear again the songbird's sweet melodious tone
Meet me in the moonlight alone

The dusky light, the day is losing
Orchids, poppies, black-eyed Susan
The earth and sky that melts with flesh and bone
Meet me in the moonlight alone

The air is thick and heavy
All along the levee
Where the geese into the countryside have flown
Meet me in the moonlight alone

Well, I'm preachin' peace and harmony
The blessings of tranquility
Floating like a dream across the floor
I'll take you 'cross the river dear
You've no need to linger here
Draw the blinds, step outside the door

月光

四季轮转
我的心在哀哀期盼
再次听到夜莺甜蜜的旋律
独自来月光下与我相见

黄昏的光，白昼在逝去
兰花、罂粟、黑眼苏珊
大地和天空骨肉相连
独自来月光下与我相见

空气浓湿沉重
沿着河堤翻涌
堤上的大雁飞进乡野
独自来月光下与我相见

哦，我颂扬和谐与和平
这一派安宁是神的恩宠
宛如一个梦漂过地面
亲爱的我将渡你到对岸
再没必要在这儿徘徊
拉上百叶窗，走出门外

The clouds are turnin' crimson
The leaves fall from the limbs an'
The branches cast their shadows over stone
Meet me in the moonlight alone

The boulevards of Cypress trees
The masquerades of birds and bees
The petals, pink and white, the wind has blown
Meet me in the moonlight alone

The trailing moss and mystic glow
Purple blossoms soft as snow
Step up and drop the coin right into the slot
The fading light of sunset glowed
It's crowded on the narrow road
Who cares whether you forgive me or not

My pulse is runnin' through my palm
The sharp hills are rising from
The yellow fields with twisted oaks that groan
Meet me in the moonlight alone

云彩渐渐变成深红色
落叶在四面枝头飘着
枝条将身影投在岩石上
独自来月光下与我相见

林荫大道柏树森森
鸟和蜜蜂的化装舞会
风吹过粉的白的花瓣
独自来月光下与我相见

蔓生的青苔，神秘的辉光
紫色花温柔得像雪一样
上前将分币塞进投币口
夕阳的余晖炉火般深幽
狭路上人群熙熙攘攘
谁会在意你是否将我原谅

我的心跳奔跑着穿过掌心
群山尖利自金黄原野升腾
扭动的橡树低低呼唤
独自来月光下与我相见

HONEST WITH ME

Well, I'm stranded in the city that never sleeps
Some of these women they just give me the creeps
I'm avoidin' the Southside the best I can
These memories I got, they can strangle a man
Well, I came ashore in the dead of the night
Lot of things can get in the way when you're tryin' to do
    what's right
You don't understand it—my feelings for you
You'd be honest with me if only you knew

I'm not sorry for nothin' I've done
I'm glad I fought—I only wish we'd won
The Siamese twins are comin' to town
People can't wait—they're gathered around
When I left my home the sky split open wide
I never wanted to go back there—I'd rather have died
You don't understand it—my feelings for you
You'd be honest with me if only you knew

对我诚实

哦，在这不眠的城市抛锚

这里一些女人让我心里发毛

我尽可能绕开南市区

那里的记忆，足以将人吊死

哦，在夜的死寂中我登上海岸

当你尽力想做对事，就会有

　　很多阻拦

你不明白——我对你的感情

你会对我诚实，一旦你真的懂了

做过的一切我了无遗憾

很高兴我拼过——我只希望我们能赢

连体暹罗人[1]要进城了

人们迫不及待——从四面八方涌来

我离家时天空裂开了

我不会再回去——宁可去死

你不明白——我对你的感情

你会对我诚实，一旦你真的懂了

---

[1] 连体暹罗人，美国著名的连体人表演者，名叫"恩昌兄弟"（1811—1874）。

My woman got a face like a teddy bear

She's tossin' a baseball bat in the air

The meat is so tough you can't cut it with a sword

I'm crashin' my car, trunk first into the boards

You say my eyes are pretty and my smile is nice

Well, I'll sell it to ya at a reduced price

You don't understand it—my feelings for you

You'd be honest with me if only you knew

Some things are too terrible to be true

I won't come here no more if it bothers you

The Southern Pacific leaving at nine forty-five

I'm having a hard time believin' some people were ever alive

I'm stark naked, but I don't care

I'm going off into the woods, I'm huntin' bare

You don't understand it—my feelings for you

Well, you'd be honest with me if only you knew

I'm here to create the new imperial empire

I'm going to do whatever circumstances require

I care so much for you—didn't think that I could

I can't tell my heart that you're no good

我女人长了张泰迪熊脸

她在空中挥舞球棒

那肉太硬了，你用剑都剁不动

我猛撞着我的车，后厢先进了表盘

你说我的眼好看我的笑容很美

哦，我可以便宜卖给你

你不明白——我对你的感情

你会对我诚实，一旦你真的懂了

有些事太可怕了，简直不像真的

我不会再来，如果这让你烦心

"南太平洋"[1] 号九点四十五分发车

实在难以置信有些人居然活过

我一丝都不挂，可是我不在乎

我要到丛林去，我打猎时光屁股[2]

你不明白——我对你的感情

你会对我诚实，一旦你真的懂了

我来这儿是要建一个新帝国

只要情势需要，什么我都会做

我这么在乎你——这我也没想到

不会在心里念你的不好

---

[1] "南太平洋"，美国铁路公司，有列车从中西部开往加州。

[2] 光屁股（bare）与熊（bear）谐音，对应上一段的"我女人长了张泰迪熊脸"，暗示做爱。

Well, my parents they warned me not to waste my years

And I still got their advice oozing out of my ears

You don't understand it—my feelings for you

Well, you'd be honest with me if only you knew

哦，父母告诫我不要虚度光阴
迄今这耳朵里仍在渗出他们的叮咛
你不明白——我对你的感情
你会对我诚实，一旦你真的懂了

PO' BOY

Man comes to the door—I say, "For whom are you looking?"
He says, "Your wife." I say, "She's busy in the kitchen cookin'."
Poor boy, where you been?
I already tol' you—won't tell you again

I say, "How much you want for that?" I go into the store
The man says, "Three dollars." "All right," I say, "Will you
    take four?"
Poor boy, never say die
Things will be all right by and by

Been workin' on the mainline—workin' like the devil
The game is the same—it's just up on a different level
Poor boy, dressed in black
Police at your back

Poor boy in a red hot town
Out beyond the twinklin' stars
Ridin' first class trains—making the rounds
Tryin' to keep from fallin' between the cars

可怜的孩子

有人来到门前——我说："你找谁？"
他说："你妻子。"我说："她在厨房忙着。"
可怜的孩子，你去哪儿了？
我已经跟你说过——不想再说

我走进商店，我说："那个要多少钱？"
那人说："三块。""好吧，"我说，"四块
　　干不干？"
可怜的孩子，永不言弃
一切都会好，在不久的后世

在铁路干线干活——累得像鬼
游戏总是一样——只是层次不同
可怜的孩子，穿一身黑
警察在你身后

可怜的孩子在火烫的城
远过那些闪烁的星
坐头等列车——兜着圈子
小心在车厢间摔倒

Othello told Desdemona, "I'm cold, cover me with a blanket.

By the way, what happened to that poison wine?" She says, "I

   gave it to you, you drank it."

Poor boy, layin' 'em straight

Pickin' up the cherries fallin' off the plate

Time and love has branded me with its claws

Had to go to Florida, dodgin' them Georgia laws

Poor boy, sitting in the gloom

Calls down to room service, says, "Send up a room."

My mother was a daughter of a wealthy farmer

My father was a traveling salesman, I never met him

When my mother died, my uncle took me in—he ran

   a funeral parlor

He did a lot of nice things for me and I won't forget him

All I know is that I'm thrilled by your kiss

I don't know any more than this

Poor boy, pickin' up sticks

Build ya a house out of mortar and bricks

Knockin' on the door, I say, "Who is it

奥赛罗对苔丝德蒙娜 [1] 说："我冷，给我盖床毯子。
对了，那毒酒怎么回事？" 她说："我给你了，
　你喝了。"
可怜的孩子，把它们摆齐
将掉在盘外的樱桃捡起

时间和爱用爪子给我盖了印
我只好跑路去佛罗里达，避开佐治亚法令
可怜的孩子，坐在昏黑里
拨打客房服务，说："送个房间上来。"

我母亲是富农的女儿
父亲是个旅行推销员，我没见过他
我母亲死后，舅舅带我——他开了家
　殡仪馆
为我做了许多好事，我不会忘记他

我只知道你的吻使我战栗
除此之外我一无所知
可怜的孩子，捡起树枝
用砂浆和砖块给你盖座房子

有人敲门，我说："谁？

----

[1] 奥赛罗、苔丝德蒙娜，莎士比亚戏剧《奥赛罗》中的男女主人公，
　此对话与该剧无关。

and where are you from?"

Man says, "Freddy!" I say, "Freddy who?" He says, "Freddy or

not here I come."

Poor boy, 'neath the stars that shine

Washin' them dishes, feedin' them swine

从哪儿来？"

来人说："弗雷迪！"我说："弗雷迪谁？"他说：
　"弗雷迪好没好，我来了。"[1]

可怜的孩子，上面群星闪烁

给他们洗盘子，给他们喂猪

---

[1] 英文笑话，"弗雷迪"（Freddy）谐音"准备好"（ready）。

CRY A WHILE

Well, I had to go down and see a guy named Mr. Goldsmith

A nasty, dirty, double-crossin', back-stabbin' phony I didn't
　　wanna have to be dealin' with

But I did it for you and all you gave me was a smile

Well, I cried for you—now it's your turn to cry awhile

I don't carry dead weight—I'm no flash in the pan

All right, I'll set you straight, can't you see I'm a union man?

I'm lettin' the cat out of the cage, I'm keeping a low profile

Well, I cried for you—now it's your turn, you can cry awhile

Feel like a fighting rooster—feel better than I ever felt

But the Pennsylvania line's in an awful mess and the Denver
　　road is about to melt

I went to the church house, every day I go an extra mile

Well, I cried for you—now it's your turn, you can cry awhile

Last night 'cross the alley there was a pounding on the walls

哭会儿

哦，我得下去见所谓的戈德史密斯[1]先生

一个肮脏、下流、阳奉阴违、背后插刀的骗子

  我才懒得打交道

但我这么做是为了你而你只给了我一个微笑

哦，我为你哭过——现在轮到你哭会儿

我扛不动这死沉玩意儿——我不是昙花一现

好吧，我澄清一下，你没看出我是工会会员？

我放猫出笼[2]，我保持低调

哦，我为你哭过——现在轮到你了，你可以哭会儿

感觉像一只斗鸡——从没这么爽过

但宾夕法尼亚线一团糟，丹佛路即将

  融化

我去了教堂，每一天多走一英里

哦，我为你哭过——现在轮到你了，你可以哭会儿

昨晚巷子那边传来砸墙的嗵嗵响

---

[1] 戈德史密斯，指哈维·戈德史密斯，英国著名摇滚演唱会策划人。

[2] 放猫出笼，改自习语"让猫从口袋里出来"——意为无意中泄露机密、泄露天机。

It must have been Don Pasqualli makin' a two A.M. booty call
To break a trusting heart like mine was just your style
Well, I cried for you—now it's your turn to cry awhile

I'm on the fringes of the night, fighting back tears that I can't
    control
Some people they ain't human, they got no heart or soul
Well, I'm crying to the Lord—I'm tryin' to be meek and mild
Yes, I cried for you—now it's your turn, you can cry awhile

Well, there's preachers in the pulpits and babies in the cribs
I'm longin' for that sweet fat that sticks to your ribs
I'm gonna buy me a barrel of whiskey—I'll die before I turn
    senile
Well, I cried for you—now it's your turn, you can cry awhile

Well, you bet on a horse and it ran on the wrong way
I always said you'd be sorry and today could be the day
I might need a good lawyer, could be your funeral, my trial
Well, I cried for you—now it's your turn, you can cry awhile

一定是帕斯夸莱老爷[1]凌晨两点找人上床
碾碎一颗像我这样的真心就是你的作风
哦，我为你哭过——现在轮到你哭会儿

我在夜的边缘，强忍着无法控制的
　　眼泪
有些人不是人，他们没有心和魂
哦，我呼喊着上帝——尽量地温柔又驯顺
是的，我为你哭过——现在轮到你了，你可以哭会儿

哦，牧师在讲坛，宝宝在摇篮
我渴望着那块紧贴你肋骨的美肉
我要买桶威士忌——赶在我老朽之前
　　死去
哦，我为你哭过——现在轮到你了，你可以哭会儿

哦，你赌了一匹马，结果它跑错道
我一直说你会后悔，今天日子到了
我可能需要个好律师，为你的葬礼、我的审判
哦，我为你哭过——现在轮到你了，你可以哭会儿

───────────

[1] 帕斯夸莱老爷，意大利作曲家多尼采蒂同名歌剧中的一个单身老
　　地主。

SUGAR BABY

I got my back to the sun 'cause the light is too intense
I can see what everybody in the world is up against
You can't turn back—you can't come back, sometimes we push
   too far
One day you'll open up your eyes and you'll see where we are

Sugar Baby get on down the road
You ain't got no brains, no how
You went years without me
Might as well keep going now

Some of these bootleggers, they make pretty good stuff
Plenty of places to hide things here if you wanna hide 'em
   bad enough
I'm staying with Aunt Sally, but you know, she's not really
   my aunt
Some of these memories you can learn to live with and some of
   them you can't

Sugar Baby get on down the line
You ain't got no brains, no how
You went years without me

糖宝宝

我背对太阳因为光实在太强
我看得清楚这世上每人究竟面对着什么
你不能回头——回不来了，有时我们
　　推进得太远
某天你一睁眼就发现，我们已经到了哪里

糖宝宝，沿这条道走下去
你没有头脑，完全就没有
你已经走了多年没我陪伴
不妨就这样，继续走下去

这些私录贼，有时真弄出了好玩意儿
这里有的是地方藏，只要你真的
　　可劲儿装
我跟莎莉姨在一起，不过你知道，她不真的
　　是我姨
这些回忆有的你能学着接受有的完全
　　没戏

糖宝宝，沿这条道走下去
你没有头脑，完全就没有
你已经走了多年没我陪伴

You might as well keep going now

The ladies in Darktown, they're doing the Darktown Strut
You always got to be prepared but you never know for what
There ain't no limit to the amount of trouble women bring
Love is pleasing, love is teasing, love's not an evil thing

Sugar Baby, get on down the road
You ain't got no brains, no how
You went years without me
You might as well keep going now

Every moment of existence seems like some dirty trick
Happiness can come suddenly and leave just as quick
Any minute of the day the bubble could burst
Try to make things better for someone, sometimes you just end
    up making it a thousand times worse

Sugar Baby, get on down the road
You ain't got no brains, no how
You went years without me
Might as well keep going now

Your charms have broken many a heart and mine is surely one
You got a way of tearing a world apart, love, see what you done
Just as sure as we're living, just as sure as you're born

不妨就这样，继续走下去

黑暗城的女士，秀着黑暗城的阔步
你总是时刻准备却从不知道为何
女人们带来的烦恼无休无止
爱是愉悦，爱是挑逗，爱不是坏事

糖宝宝，沿这条道走下去
你没有头脑，完全就没有
你已经走了多年没我陪伴
不妨就这样，继续走下去

存在的每一刻都像是肮脏的把戏
幸福会骤然降临然后又猝然消失
一天中每一分钟泡沫都可能破灭
尽可能为人把事办好吧，虽然到头来有时
　　千倍地坏事儿

糖宝宝，沿这条道走下去
你没有头脑，完全就没有
你已经走了多年没我陪伴
不妨就这样，继续走下去

你的魅力伤了许多人的心，我也是其中一个
你有办法撕裂世界，亲爱的，瞧瞧你都干了什么
就像我们活着一样确然，像你出生一样确然

Look up, look up—seek your Maker—'fore Gabriel
   blows his horn

Sugar Baby, get on down the line
You ain't got no sense, no how
You went years without me
Might as well keep going now

看上面，看上面——寻你的造物主——趁加百列
　　吹响号角之前

糖宝宝，沿这条道走下去
你没有理智，完全就没有
你已经走了多年没我陪伴
不妨就这样，继续走下去

'CROSS THE GREEN MOUNTAIN
(FROM THE FILM *GODS AND GENERALS*)

I crossed the green mountain, I slept by the stream

Heaven blazin' in my head, I dreamt a monstrous dream

Something came up out of the sea

Swept through the land of the rich and the free

I look into the eyes of my merciful friend

And then I ask myself, is this the end?

Memories linger, sad yet sweet

And I think of the souls in heaven who will meet

Altars are burning with flames falling wide

The foe has crossed over from the other side

They tip their caps from the top of the hill

You can feel them come, more brave blood to spill

Along the dim Atlantic line

The ravaged land lies for miles behind

越过青青山岭 [1]

（电影《众神与将军》插曲）

我越过青青山岭，宿在那溪流之滨

天空在颅内燃烧，我做了个可怕的梦

海里来了怪异之物

扫掠过富足者和自由人的大地

我凝望着朋友临终的眼

然后问自己，这就是终点？

记忆盘桓，悲伤却甜蜜

我想着那灵魂，到了天堂将会相遇

祭坛被四面飞落的火焰点燃

敌人从另一面过河上岸

在山顶他们触帽敬礼

你能感到大敌压境，更多热血上涌

沿着昏暗的大西洋线

遍地焦土数英里绵延

---

[1] 这首歌所述内容与影片情节有关。《众神与将军》塑造了美国南北战争初期双方忠勇将士的群像，较倾向于南军的意识形态，尤其关注了南军名将"石墙"杰克逊的传奇生涯。

The light's comin' forward and the streets are broad
All must yield to the avenging God

The world is old, the world is gray
Lessons of life can't be learned in a day
I watch and I wait and I listen while I stand
To the music that comes from a far better land

Close the eyes of our Captain, peace may he know
His long night is done, the great leader is laid low
He was ready to fall, he was quick to defend
Killed outright he was by his own men

It's the last day's last hour of the last happy year
I feel that the unknown world is so near
Pride will vanish and glory will rot
But virtue lives and cannot be forgot

The bells of evening have rung
There's blasphemy on every tongue
Let them say that I walked in fair nature's light
And that I was loyal to truth and to right

Serve God and be cheerful, look upward beyond
Beyond the darkness that masks the surprises of dawn
In the deep green grasses of the blood stained wood

光明向前，街道宽阔
一切须听命那复仇之神

世界古老，世界灰暗
人生的课程不可能一天学完
我观察我等待我谛听当我坚守时
听那来自更美好土地的乐音

阖上我们队长的眼，愿他安息
他的长夜已终，伟大领袖长眠地底
他做好了沦陷准备，他迅速反击
却被自己人击中，当场死去

这是最后的欢乐岁月的最后一天的最后时辰
我感到那个未知世界是如此之近
骄傲会消失，荣耀将锈蚀
但善义长存，永远铭记

晚钟已经敲响
每条唇舌都在亵渎神
让他们说吧，说我行于自然公正之光
说我忠于真理和正义

侍奉上帝而喜乐，向天上看
越过遮蔽惊喜黎明的黑暗
在鲜血染红的林中，那碧绿的草地上

They never dreamed of surrendering. They fell where they stood

Stars fell over Alabama, I saw each star
You're walkin' in dreams whoever you are
Chilled are the skies, keen is the frost
The ground's froze hard and the morning is lost

A letter to mother came today
Gunshot wound to the breast is what it did say
But he'll be better soon he's in a hospital bed
But he'll never be better, he's already dead

I'm ten miles outside the city and I'm lifted away
In an ancient light that is not of day
They were calm, they were blunt, we knew 'em all too well
We loved each other more than we ever dared to tell

他们从未想过投降。他们倒在站立的地方

星星陨落亚拉巴马，我看见每颗星
无论你是谁，你都是行走于梦境
九霄冷彻，寒霜凛冽
大地冰冻而早晨不再来临

给母亲的信今天到了
胸口受了枪伤，信上说
说他很快会好起来，他在医院病床上
但他不会好起来了，他已经死了 [1]

我在城外十英里，我被人抬着走
照亮我的是旧时的光，不是来自这白昼
他们平静，他们直率，我们对他们太了解
我们彼此深爱，胜过最大胆的表白

---

[1] "石墙"杰克逊以防守反击著称，在一次夜巡中却被己方误击，重伤
而死。

WAITIN' FOR YOU

(FROM THE FILM *DIVINE SECRETS OF THE YA-YA SISTERHOOD*)

I never dreamed there could be someone made just for me

I'm not letting her have her way

I come here to see what she has to say

Oh, the poor gal always wins the day

I'm staying ahead of the game, she's doing the same

And the whiskey's flying into my head

The fiddler's arm has gone dead

And talk is beginning to spread

When did our love go bad?

Whatever happened to the best friend that I had?

Been so long since I held you tight

Been so long since we said goodnight

The taste of tears is bittersweet

When you're near me, my heart forgets to beat

You're there every night among the good and the true

And I'll be around, waitin' for you

The king of them all is starting to fall

I lost my gal at the boatman's ball

等你
（电影《丫丫姐妹们的神圣秘密》插曲）

做梦也想不到有个人是为我量身定做
我不会让她想哪出就哪出
我来这儿看看她有什么要说
啊，可怜的姑娘总是有赢无输
比赛中我一路领先，她也是同样局面
然后威士忌飘入我脑海
提琴手的胳膊已玩儿完
而谈话开始漫无边际

我们的爱从何时开始变味儿？
我最好的朋友到底出了啥事儿？
很久没抱紧你了
很久没道晚安了
眼泪的滋味又甜又涩
当你靠近我，我的心忘记了跳跃
每夜每夜你都在真善之际
而我会在鞍前马后，等你

他们的王开始倒台
我在船夫舞会失去了我的女孩

The night has a thousand hearts and eyes

Hope may vanish but it never dies

I'll see you tomorrow when freedom rings

I'm gonna stay on top of things

It's the middle of the summer and the moon is blue

I'll be around waitin' for you

Another deal gone down, another man done gone

You put up with it all and you carry on

Something holding you back but you'll come through

I'd bet the world and everything in it on you

Happiness is but a state of mind

Anytime you want you can cross the state line

You don't need to be rich or well-to-do

I'll be around waitin' for you

黑夜有一千颗心一千只眼
希望会破灭但希望永不会完蛋
明天自由钟声响起时我们会再见
届时我会掌控局面
现在是盛夏，月亮蓝莹莹
我会在鞍前马后等你

又一单输掉，又一人出局
你忍受一切，你继续坚持
有些事拖你回头但你会穿越而过
我在你身上押上了世界和一切一切
幸福不过是种心态
你随时想起都可以跨过边界
你没必要发财没必要富裕
我会在鞍前马后等你

MODERN TIMES
摩登时代

1. Lost John, sitting on the railroad track / Something's out of whack
   Blues this morning falling down like hail
   Gonna leave a greasy trail

2. Gonna travel the world is what I'm going to do / then come back and see you
   Days creep by, each one feels like a year (= many many years)
   So many things come to nothing (could I love...

3. I'm the oldest son of a crazy man / I'm in a cowboy band
   Got a pile of sins to pay for me / And got time to hide
   I'd walk thru a blazing fire badly if I knew you was on the other side

4. Going where the Southern crosses the yellow Dog / to get away from those demagogues
   And those bad luck women that stick / tighter like glue
   Always getting in the way when there's work to do

5. Dr. Frankenstein's still up there at his castle on the hill
   Albert in the graveyard, Frankie's raising hell
   I'm beginning to believe (empty text) what the scriptures tell
   let's go down (let's go down to Jacksonville) went psycho hell
   Stopping all my thoughts before this start tchou win...
   cowboy at em once once only
   up there still (with the moon's fine shell) she's a
   I'm going to Jackson-ville) (cathouse woman had -- there saving all day em)

6. She says "(look out Daddy, don't wanna to tear your pants! / you could get wrecked in this deuce"
   They say that whiskey'll kill ya but / I don't think it will
   You went away and left the bit / I believe you love me still

7. It's getting light outside, the temperature dropped / I think the rain has stopped
   I'm going to kneel again come to grips with fate
   When I'm thru with you, you'll learn how to keep your business straight
   It's win two like (been) It can (turn the worm begun) for all

8. The judge is comin', all rise / lift up your eyes
   I went to the river, threw away my dice
   Before you call me they dirty names, you better think twice

9. Don't know why my baby been cooked so good before / I don't have to wonder no more
   She been cookin' see deep, find it's gonna take me all night
   I can't eat it all eat up in a single bite
   I'm sweet love his clean tonight) won-

10. Today I cry stand in faith And raise / the voice of praise
    My heart would burn go astray / they would keep go astray?
    A lifetime with you is like some heavenly day
    (You're inside all in Every kind of grief gives way / I could keep em go away — should be Anyother wrong

11. Everything I've ever known to be right has been proven wrong / I'll be driftin' Along
    I went to the dance / wore out my shoes
    She says "don't worry ('bout it) Daddy, don't you know you can't lose"
    A cathouse woman's a god gifted man go head to head—
    showy baby today

12. The bright spark of the steady lights / has veiled today's distracting sights
    I know you'd never throw me down (I'll be livin' you when you whisper from the ground)
    When you die, I'll keep hanging around — (that dime)
    (no where in sight) with I'm livin' many lives — (I was born on high ground I'm stuck with you)
    (never thrown you down)

13. Lost John — 1st verse —

《"爱与窃"》推出5年后，2006年8月29日，迪伦第32张录音室专辑《摩登时代》由哥伦比亚唱片公司发行，成为中老年迪伦第3张广受好评的作品。65岁的歌坛前辈带着新作横扫各国排行榜，这使迪伦成为登顶《公告牌》专辑榜最年长的人。

　　然而，《摩登时代》比《"爱与窃"》引来了更多非议。专辑中这些老布鲁斯、老摇滚乐、老乡村音乐和老民歌，一方面古风扑面，一方面被考据派挖出更多"窃取"的印迹，几乎没有哪首歌没用到前人的旋律、诗句、副歌或编曲。

　　虽然音乐方面偶有相似，但全部歌曲都有迪伦全新创作的歌词支撑。相较之下，更令人疑虑的倒是歌词方面的"撞车"。唱片骑师斯科特·瓦尔穆特（Scott Warmuth）在《纽约时报》撰文指出，《摩登时代》中的多首歌词，至少有10处诗句和短语，与美国南北战争时期诗人亨利·蒂姆罗德（Henry Timrod）的词句相似，但唱片册文案中却找不到蒂姆罗德的名字。

　　新西兰《尼尔森邮报》则刊登了本国诗人克利夫·费尔（Cliff Fell）的文章，指出《摩登时代》中的5首歌

《山上的雷霆》《劳工蓝调 2 号》《不作声》《大堤就要决口》《灵行于水上》，各有一句歌词与古罗马诗人奥维德的诗句几乎一模一样。

　　但费尔并不认为这是抄袭，只觉得是借用。针对"剽窃非议"，美国诗歌基金会的罗伯特·波利托（Robert Polito）提醒众人，勿将"艺术与学术论文"混为一谈。

　　通观全辑，古老的黑人布鲁斯，再一次成为触发迪伦灵感的"验方"，10 首歌曲充满神秘的诗意，也激发今人的想象。《摩登时代》看起来是古旧的，却指向当代和未来。还很少有人指出，它有仿佛属于过去的背景，有众多古老的意象，有大致属于黑人布鲁斯的文体，与此同时，却有布鲁斯历史上从未有过的宽广胸怀和雄伟体量。

　　《山上的雷霆》《灵行于水上》《劳工蓝调 2 号》《妮蒂·摩尔》《不作声》都是大作，具有汹涌澎湃的海量信息和如山洪、如风雷般的雄奇气势。一些歌曲，比如《山上的雷霆》和《劳工蓝调 2 号》，其宏阔而错综复杂的意味，是这样的文体从未承载过的。

　　《山上的雷霆》《灵行于水上》再次书写《圣经》启示，却有比前作更迂回、幽深乃至绝望的重重暗道。表面上看，《妮蒂·摩尔》在表达对一个女人的思念，实则讲述了跨越美国历史一两百年、黑白不同种族、数代重叠的故事。《不作声》被置于终曲，如专辑《被遗忘的时光》中的《高地》一样，映射着一个独行者最后的孤旅。只是这一次，他要去的高地不在远方，道路竟切近如斯，仿佛不经意一转，即进入了伊甸园。但是这里却似乎离目的地更远，更加疑云重重，充满了解不开的仙根。"空无一人，园丁也已离去"。然而，这独行者却更多了几分笃定和沉静，仍怀憧憬，显现出谨慎的乐观。

即使那些体裁单纯、结构看似更小、篇幅显然更短的歌曲，比如《终有一天宝贝》《契约达成的时候》《翻来覆去》《大堤就要决口》《地平线另一边》，其内涵也纵贯人的一生。无论歌曲长短，这些歌词都体现出人生总结和宗教反思的意识，指向人生道路尽头甚至累世的迷局。苦行者怀着悲苦而又火热的心走向世界终点，想象着越过地平线到另一边去寻求答案。在写作状态上，它不是沉思也不是抒情，而是一种贯通了毕生阅历和终身思虑、在一种意念凝聚下的入神的喷涌，令人惊叹地发散着老一辈文艺大师那暮年的睿智和敏锐的冷静。作为一位老人，迪伦找到了一种新的表达方式，也将为后来者提供路标和参照。

再一次，整张专辑是迪伦与他的巡演乐队一起录制的。2005年一整年，这支乐队都在"永不停止的巡演"中与迪伦一起演出。2006年1月下旬至2月初，他们在纽约一家歌剧院排练，然后在2月的最后3周，在纽约克林顿录音室，以现场方式录出了专辑中的全部歌曲。

在完成这张专辑的5年间，迪伦还撰写了自传《编年史》（第一卷），参与了其传记电影《没有方向的家》（*No Direction Home*，马丁·斯科塞斯执导）的制作。

THUNDER ON THE MOUNTAIN

Thunder on the mountain, fires on the moon
There's a ruckus in the alley and the sun will be here soon
Today's the day, gonna grab my trombone and blow
Well, there's hot stuff here and it's everywhere I go
I was thinkin' 'bout Alicia Keys, couldn't keep from crying
When she was born in Hell's Kitchen, I was living
    down the line
I'm wondering where in the world Alicia Keys could be
I been looking for her even clear through Tennessee
Feel like my soul is beginning to expand
Look into my heart and you will sort of understand
You brought me here, now you're trying to run me away
The writing's on the wall, come read it, come see what it say

Thunder on the mountain, rolling like a drum
Gonna sleep over there, that's where the music coming from
I don't need any guide, I already know the way
Remember this, I'm your servant both night and day
The pistols are poppin' and the power is down

山上的雷霆

山上的雷霆，月亮上的火焰
巷子开始喧闹，太阳即将出现
今天就是这一天，我要抓起长号吹响
哦，满眼是烫手货，走哪儿都是惹火姑娘
我想起艾丽西亚·凯斯 [1]，忍不住哭出声来
她在地狱厨房 [2] 出生时，我就住在
　那一带
我在想艾丽西亚·凯斯到底去了哪里
为了找她我已经翻遍整个田纳西
感觉我的灵魂正在展开
看进我的心你就会有点明白
你把我带到这儿，现在又极力催我远离
那墙上有字迹，去读读吧，看它写了什么话语

山上的雷霆，滚滚如鼓击
必须到那儿睡，音乐就来自那里
我不需要向导，我已经认得路
记住吧，我是你的仆人无论日升日暮
手枪砰砰响，电力系统中断

---

[1]　艾丽西亚·凯斯（1981—），美国女歌手。
[2]　地狱厨房，纽约市曼哈顿西岸的一个地区。

I'd like to try somethin' but I'm so far from town

The sun keeps shinin' and the North Wind keeps picking up
  speed

Gonna forget about myself for a while, gonna go out and see
  what others need

I've been sitting down studying the art of love

I think it will fit me like a glove

I want some real good woman to do just what I say

Everybody got to wonder what's the matter with this cruel
  world today

Thunder on the mountain rolling to the ground

Gonna get up in the morning walk the hard road down

Some sweet day I'll stand beside my king

I wouldn't betray your love or any other thing

Gonna raise me an army, some tough sons of bitches

I'll recruit my army from the orphanages

I been to St. Herman's church and I've said my religious vows

I've sucked the milk out of a thousand cows

I got the porkchops, she got the pie

She ain't no angel and neither am I

Shame on your greed, shame on your wicked schemes

I'll say this, I don't give a damn about your dreams

Thunder on the mountain heavy as can be

Mean old twister bearing down on me

我想做点什么，但离市区太远
太阳依旧照耀而北风愈加
　　猛烈
要暂时忘却自己，出去看
　　别人需要什么
我一直坐这儿研习爱的技艺
我想它就像手套一样适合我
我想要个真正的好女人一切照我说的做
每个人都困惑眼下这残酷的世界
　　究竟怎么了

山上的雷霆滚落在地上
我将一早起身，踏上艰难路走向前方
某个甜美日子我会站在国王身边
你的爱及其他我都不会背叛
我将拉起一支大军，一帮婊子养的壮丁
我将从孤儿院招募我的人
我去过圣赫尔曼教堂在教上立过誓
我吸过一千头奶牛的乳汁
我拿了猪排，她拿了派
她不是天使我也不是
可耻啊你的贪，可耻啊你的阴谋诡计
我必须说，我才不在乎你的什么梦想呢

山上的雷霆沉重无比
凶猛的老龙卷风步步紧逼

All the ladies of Washington scrambling to get out of town

Looks like something bad gonna happen, better roll your
airplane down

Everybody's going and I want to go too

Don't wanna take a chance with somebody new

I did all I could and I did it right there and then

I've already confessed—no need to confess again

Gonna make a lot of money, gonna go up north

I'll plant and I'll harvest what the earth brings forth

The hammer's on the table, the pitchfork's on the shelf

For the love of God, you ought to take pity on yourself

华盛顿众女士争相出城
看来大事不妙，你的飞机最好
　　拉低飞行
人人都在跑我也想逃离
不想跟新人冒险赌运气
我竭尽所能在那儿立即行事
已经忏悔过了——没必要还去
要赚大钱，要去北方
将去种地，收获大地所育
锤子在桌上，干草叉在架上
看在上帝分上，你须怜悯自己

SPIRIT ON THE WATER

Spirit on the water

Darkness on the face of the deep

I keep thinking about you baby

I can't hardly sleep

I'm traveling by land

Traveling through the dawn of day

You're always on my mind

I can't stay away

I'd forgotten about you

Then you turned up again

I always knew

That we were meant to be more than friends

When you are near

It's just as plain as it can be

I'm wild about you, gal

You ought to be a fool about me

Can't explain

The sources of this hidden pain

You burned your way into my heart

You got the key to my brain

I've been trampling through mud

灵行于水上

灵行于水上
渊面黑暗
我想你宝贝
难以成眠
我在陆路旅行
穿越晨曦
你一直在我心里
挥之不去
一度我忘记你
然后你再度出现
我始终都明白
你我不只朋友而已
当你就在近旁
这事实简单无比
我为你疯狂，姑娘
你也理应为我痴迷

无从解释
这隐痛缘起
你燃烧着进入我心
你有我大脑的钥匙
我在泥泞中跋涉

Praying to the powers above

I'm sweating blood

You got a face that begs for love

Life without you

Doesn't mean a thing to me

If I can't have you

I'll throw my love into the deep blue sea

Sometimes I wonder

Why you can't treat me right

You do good all day

Then you do wrong all night

When you're with me

I'm a thousand times happier than I could ever say

What does it matter

What price I pay

They brag about your sugar

Brag about it all over town

Put some sugar in my bowl

I feel like laying down

I'm pale as a ghost

Holding a blossom on a stem

You ever seen a ghost? No

But you have heard of them

祈求天上的力量

我身上流着汗血 [1]

你有一张乞爱脸庞

这一生若没有你

人生便无意义

如果不能拥有你

我将把爱抛入海底

有时我实在困惑

为何你不好好待我

白天你样样都好

夜晚你一错再错

你和我一起时

我千倍的快乐无法言说

至于我付出什么代价

那又有什么关系

他们吹捧你的糖

吹得全城沸沸扬扬

给我碗里来点儿吧

我也想要躺一躺

我苍白得像个幽魂

手捏一枝花的花茎

你见过幽魂吗？没有

可你总听说过它们

---

[1] "流着汗血"，sweat blood，英语中寓意"累死累活地干，忧虑万分"。

I hear your name

Ringing up and down the line

I'm saying it plain

These ties are strong enough to bind

I been in a brawl

Now I'm feeling the wall

I'm going away baby

I won't be back 'til fall

High on the hill

You can carry all my thoughts with you

You've numbed my will

This love could tear me in two

I wanna be with you in paradise

And it seems so unfair

I can't go back to paradise no more

I killed a man back there

You think I'm over the hill

You think I'm past my prime

Let me see what you got

We can have a whoppin' good time

我听见你的名字
在我耳边起起伏伏
我话说得很明白了
这些纽带足够牢固

我一直吵吵嚷嚷
现在感觉撞了墙
我得走了宝贝
秋天前不会再回
从那高山之巅
你可以拿去我的思念
你麻木了我的意志
这爱能把我撕成两半
我想和你去天堂
而这似乎不公平
我再也回不了天堂
我背负了一条人命
你以为我过了巅峰
你以为我风光不再
让我瞧瞧你有什么
我们会玩得非常愉快

ROLLIN' AND TUMBLIN'

I rolled and I tumbled, I cried the whole night long
I rolled and I tumbled, I cried the whole night long
Woke up this mornin', I must have bet my money wrong

I got troubles so hard, I can't stand the strain
I got troubles so hard, I just can't stand the strain
Some young lazy slut has charmed away my brains

The landscape is glowin', gleamin' in the golden light of day
The landscape is glowin', gleamin' in the gold light of day
I ain't holding nothin' back now, I ain't standin' in
    anybody's way

I'm flat out spent, this woman been drivin' me to tears
I'm flat out spent, this woman she been drivin' me to tears
This woman so crazy, I swear I ain't gonna touch another one
    for years

Well, the warm weather is comin' and the buds are on the vine
The warm weather's comin', the buds are on the vine
Ain't nothing so depressing as trying to satisfy
    this woman of mine

翻来覆去

我翻来覆去，哭了整整一夜
我翻来覆去，哭了整整一夜
早晨醒过来，我一定是下错了注

我惹下大麻烦了，实在受不了
我惹下大麻烦了，实在是受不了
一个又嫩又懒的小浪货弄得我五迷三道

风景在白天的金色光线里闪闪亮
风景在白天的纯金光线里闪闪亮
现在我啥事不瞒，谁的道
　　都不挡

我筋疲力尽了，这女人害得我哭
我筋疲力尽了，这女人她害得我哭
这女人太疯狂，我发誓这几年不再
　　碰别人

哦，暖和天来了葡萄藤打了苞
暖和天来了，葡萄藤打了苞
没什么比尽力满足这个女人更
　　使人发愁

I got up this mornin', saw the rising sun return

Well, I got up this mornin', seen the rising sun return

Sooner or later you too shall burn

The night's filled with shadows, the years are filled with early
doom

The night's filled with shadows, the years are filled with early
doom

I've been conjuring up all these long dead souls from their
crumblin' tombs

Let's forgive each other darlin', let's go down to the greenwood
glen

Let's forgive each other darlin', let's go down to the greenwood
glen

Let's put our heads together, let's put old matters to an end

Now I rolled and I tumbled and I cried the whole night long

Ah, I rolled and I tumbled, I cried the whole night long

I woke up this morning, I think I must be travelin' wrong

我早晨起身，看见朝阳回到东方
哦，我早晨起身，又看见朝阳回到东方
或早或晚你也将被灼伤

夜晚布满阴影，岁月布满
　　夭亡
夜晚布满阴影，岁月布满
　　夭亡
我一直从他们崩塌的坟墓召唤着，这些故去
　　已久的魂灵

让我们相互原谅亲爱的，让我们走下这
　　绿林幽谷
让我们相互原谅亲爱的，让我们走下这
　　绿林幽谷
让我们一同想办法，让我们给旧事一个结束

好吧我翻来覆去哭了整整一夜
啊，我翻来覆去，哭了整整一夜
早晨醒过来，我想我一定是走错了路

WHEN THE DEAL GOES DOWN

In the still of the night, in the world's ancient light
Where wisdom grows up in strife
My bewildering brain, toils in vain
Through the darkness on the pathways of life
Each invisible prayer is like a cloud in the air
Tomorrow keeps turning around
We live and we die, we know not why
But I'll be with you when the deal goes down

We eat and we drink, we feel and we think
Far down the street we stray
I laugh and I cry and I'm haunted by
Things I never meant nor wished to say
The midnight rain follows the train
We all wear the same thorny crown
Soul to soul, our shadows roll
And I'll be with you when the deal goes down

The moon gives light and shines by night
I scarcely feel the glow
We learn to live and then we forgive
O'er the road we're bound to go

契约达成的时候

在夜的静止，在世界古老的光中
智慧在纷争中长成
我晕头转向的大脑，徒劳无功
穿过黑暗走在人生小径
每个无形祈祷都像空中一朵云
明日总是再次回转
我们生生死死，我们不明所以
但契约达成的时候我会在你身边

我们吃吃喝喝，我们感受思考
在大街深处迷失
我笑我哭我困扰
为无意讲也不想讲的事
午夜之雨追着列车
我们都戴着一样的荆冠
灵魂对灵魂，我们的影子翻滚
契约达成的时候我会在你身边

月亮发出光，因夜而闪耀
我几乎感觉不到那幽亮
我们学会生活，然后宽恕
在这条必定走的路上

More frailer than the flowers, these precious hours
That keep us so tightly bound
You come to my eyes like a vision from the skies
And I'll be with you when the deal goes down

I picked up a rose and it poked through my clothes
I followed the winding stream
I heard the deafening noise, I felt transient joys
I know they're not what they seem
In this earthly domain, full of disappointment and pain
You'll never see me frown
I owe my heart to you, and that's sayin' it true
And I'll be with you when the deal goes down

比花朵更脆弱，这些珍贵时刻
将我们紧紧拥作一团
你映入我的眼就像天上幻影
契约达成的时候我会在你身边

捡拾起一枝玫瑰，它刺穿了衣裳
我顺这溪流蜿蜒而下
听到震耳的喧腾，感觉到须臾欢欣
我知道这些并非如表面所示
在这尘世间，四处都是失望和痛苦
你永远不会见我愁眉不展
我亏欠你一颗心，这是真的
契约达成的时候我会在你身边

SOMEDAY BABY

I don't care what you do, I don't care what you say
I don't care where you go or how long you stay
Someday baby, you ain't gonna worry po' me anymore

Well you take my money and you turn me out
You fill me up with nothin' but self doubt
Someday baby, you ain't gonna worry po' me anymore

When I was young, driving was my crave
You drive me so hard, almost to the grave
Someday baby, you ain't gonna worry po' me anymore

Something is the matter, my mind tied up in knots
I keep recycling the same old thoughts
Someday baby, you ain't gonna worry po' me anymore

So many good things in life I overlooked
I don't know what to do now, you got me so hooked
Someday baby, you ain't gonna worry po' me anymore

Gonna get myself together, I'm gonna ring your neck
When all else fails I'll make it a matter of self-respect

终有一天宝贝

我不介怀你的所作所为，不在意你的言谈话语
不关心你将行何处，随便你待多久
终有一天宝贝，你再不用为我操心

嗯你拿了我的钱，把我撵出门
让我心里充满对自己的疑问
终有一天宝贝，你再不用为我操心

那时候我年轻，开车上路就是渴望
你使劲儿催我，几乎将我催进坟场
终有一天宝贝，你再不用为我操心

事情出了状况，我的心纠缠百结
我盘算着一堆不变的老处方
终有一天宝贝，你再不用为我操心

生命中这么多美好我都无暇顾及
我不知现在该怎么办，你让我如此痴迷
终有一天宝贝，你再不用为我操心

我要振作起来，我要掐住你的脖子
要是怎么都不成，这问题便将关乎自尊

Someday baby, you ain't gonna worry po' me anymore

You can take your clothes, put 'm in a sack
You goin' down the road, baby and you can't come back
Someday baby, you ain't gonna worry po' me anymore

I try to be friendly, I try to be kind
Now I'm gonna drive you from your home, just like I was
   driven from mine
Someday baby, you ain't gonna worry po' me anymore

终有一天宝贝，你再不用为我操心

来拿走你的衣服，把它们装进袋子
沿路走下去宝贝，再别回来
终有一天宝贝，你再不用为我操心

我试着友善，试着好心
现在我要把你赶出你家，就像当初
　我被撵出门
终有一天宝贝，你再不用为我操心

WORKINGMANS BLUES #2

There's an evening's haze settling over the town
Starlight by the edge of the creek
The buying power of the proletariat's gone down
Money's getting shallow and weak
The place I love best is a sweet memory
It's a new path that we trod
They say low wages are a reality
If we want to compete abroad

My cruel weapons been laid back on the shelf
Come and sit down on my knee
You are dearer to me than myself
As you yourself can see
I'm listening to the steel rails hum
Got both eyes tight shut
I'm just trying to keep the hunger from
Creepin' its way into my gut

Meet me at the bottom, don't lag behind
Bring me my boots and shoes
You can hang back or fight your best on the front line
Sing a little bit of these workingman's blues

劳工蓝调 2 号

夜雾笼罩小镇
星光闪耀溪流边
无产阶级的购买力下降
金钱变得疲软
我最爱的地方已成追忆
我们踏上的是条新路径
他们说低薪已是现实
如果我们想在海外竞争

我的暴力武器已束之高阁
过来，坐我腿上来
我爱你胜过爱自己
这点你也看得明白
我听着铁轨的嗡嗡声
把两眼紧紧闭上
只想不让饥饿
爬进胃肠

到底下见我吧，别落在后面
帮我把靴子和鞋带过来
你可以退缩或在前线全力以赴
唱一点儿这劳工小曲儿

I'm sailing on back getting ready for the long haul

Leaving everything behind

If I stay here I'll lose it all

The bandits will rob me blind

I'm trying to feed my soul with thought

Gonna sleep off the rest of the day

Sometimes nobody wants what you got

Sometimes you can't give it away

I woke up this morning and sprang to my feet

Went into town on a whim

I saw my father there in the street

At least I think it was him

In the dark I hear the night birds call

The hills are rugged and steep

I sleep in the kitchen with my feet in the hall

If I told you my whole story you'd weep

Meet me at the bottom, don't lag behind

Bring me my boots and shoes

You can hang back or fight your best on the front line

Sing a little bit of these workingman's blues

They burned my barn and they stole my horse

I can't save a dime

我起帆归航，准备远征
抛开了一切
如果还留在这儿，我就会失去全部
强盗将把我洗劫
我极力用思想喂养灵魂
余暇全部用来睡觉
有时候你的货没人要
有时候你无法将它扔掉

早晨从床上一跃而起
我心血来潮跑去市中心
在街上看到我父亲
至少我认为那是他
黑暗中我听见夜鸟叫
那片山丘陡峭崎岖
我睡在厨房，脚伸在饭厅里
如果我讲给你我全部的故事，你会哭泣

到底下见我吧，别落在后面
帮我把靴子和鞋带过来
你可以退缩或在前线全力以赴
唱一点儿这劳工小曲儿

他们烧了我的谷仓，偷走我的马
我一个子儿都存不住

It's a long way down and I don't want to be forced

Into a life of continual crime

I can see for myself that the sun is sinking

O'er the banks of the deep blue sea

Tell me, am I wrong in thinking

That you have forgotten me

Now they worry and they hurry and they fuss and they fret

They waste your nights and days

Them, I will forget

You, I'll remember always

It's a cold black night and it's midsummer's eve

And the stars are spinning around

I still find it so hard to believe

That someone would kick me when I'm down

Meet me at the bottom, don't lag behind

Bring me my boots and shoes

You can hang back or fight your best on the front line

Sing a little bit of these workingman's blues

I'll be back home in a month or two

When the frost is on the vine

I'll punch my spear right straight through

Half-ways down your spine

I'll lift up my arms to the starry skies

路还长，我不想被迫走上
无休无止的犯罪之路
我能亲眼看到太阳
正在黑蓝色大海的岸边沉落
告诉我，是我想错了吗
以为你已经忘记我

现在他们担心着急，他们烦躁瞎忙活
他们浪费了你的日日夜夜
他们，我会忘却
你，我会永远记得
这是一个寒冷的黑夜，仲夏节的前夜
星星在旋转
我仍然觉得难以置信
我倒霉时，会有人对我落井下石

到底下见我吧，别落在后面
帮我把靴子和鞋带过来
你可以退缩或在前线全力以赴
唱一点儿这劳工小曲儿

一两个月后我就会回家
当葡萄藤蒙上白霜时
我将用长矛径直刺入
你中间的脊骨
我会向星空举起双臂

And pray the fugitive's prayer
I'm guessing tomorrow the sun will rise
I hope the final judgment's fair

The battle is over up in the hills
And the mist is closing in
Look at me, with all of my spoils
What did I ever win?
Gotta brand new suit and a brand new wife
I can live on rice and beans
Some people never worked a day in their life
They don't know what work even means

Meet me at the bottom, don't lag behind
Bring me my boots and shoes
You can hang back or fight your best on the front line
Sing a little bit of these workingman's blues

为逃亡者诵念祈祷词
我估计明天太阳还会升起
我希望最后的审判是公正的

山上战斗结束了
雾气正在弥合
瞧我，以这全部的战利品
我赢得什么？
一套新西装，一个新老婆
可以靠稻米和豆子过活
有些人一辈子没劳动过一天
甚至不知道劳动是何意思

到底下见我吧，别落在后面
帮我把靴子和鞋带过来
你可以退缩或在前线全力以赴
唱一点儿这劳工小曲儿

BEYOND THE HORIZON

Beyond the horizon, behind the sun

At the end of the rainbow life has only begun

In the long hours of twilight 'neath the stardust above

Beyond the horizon it is easy to love

I'm staring out the window

Of an ancient town

Petals from flowers

Falling to the ground

Beyond the horizon, in the springtime or fall

Love waits forever, for one and for all

Beyond the horizon, across the divide

'Round about midnight, we'll be on the same side

Down in the valley the water runs cold

Beyond the horizon someone's prayin' for your soul

I lost my true lover

In the dusk, in the dawn

I have to recover

Get up and go on

Beyond the horizon, beyond love's burning game

Every step that you take, I'm walking the same

地平线另一边

地平线另一边，太阳后面
彩虹的尽头，生命刚刚开始
星尘下悠长的微光里
地平线另一边，相爱容易
是在一座古镇
我凝望窗前
花瓣从花朵
落向地面
地平线另一边，春天或秋日
爱永远等待，一个和全体

地平线另一边，跨越分界线
午夜时分，我们抵达同一面
山谷中流水变得冷峭
地平线另一边，有人为你的灵魂祷告
我失去了真爱
在黄昏，在黎明
我必须恢复
爬起来继续前行
地平线另一边，超越爱情燃烧游戏
你走的每一步，我亦步亦趋

Beyond the horizon, the night winds blow

The theme of a melody from many moons ago

The bells of St. Mary, how sweetly they chime

Beyond the horizon I found you just in time

Slipping and sliding

Too late to stop

Riding and gliding

It's lonely at the top

Beyond the horizon, the sky is so blue

I've got more than a lifetime to live lovin' you

地平线另一边，夜风吹拂起
很久前的一支旋律主题
圣玛丽的钟，敲击声多美妙
地平线另一边，我及时将你找到
轻移，滑行
来不及停
驰骋，飞翔
高处寂冷
地平线另一边，长天一碧如洗
我有不止一生一世的时间爱你

NETTIE MOORE

Lost John sittin' on a railroad track
Something's out of whack
Blues this morning falling down like hail
Gonna leave a greasy trail

Gonna travel the world is what I'm gonna do
Then come back and see you
All I ever do is struggle and strive
If I don't do anybody any harm, I might make it
    back home alive

I'm the oldest son of a crazy man
I'm in a cowboy band
Got a pile of sins to pay for and I ain't got time to hide
I'd walk through a blazing fire, baby, if I knew you was on the
    other side

Oh, I miss you Nettie Moore
And my happiness is o'er
Winter's gone, the river's on the rise
I loved you then and ever shall
But there's no one here that's left to tell

妮蒂·摩尔

迷路的约翰坐在铁轨上
一些东西不对劲
早晨的蓝调像冰雹砸下
将留下油乎乎的印痕

我想要做的是去环游世界
然后再回来看你
我一直不是斗就是拼
假如我谁都没伤害，我就会
　活着回来

我是一个疯子的长子
在一支牛仔乐队混事儿
有一堆罪要偿，没时间躲闪
我会穿过火焰，宝贝，假如我知道
　你在那边

啊，我想你妮蒂·摩尔
我的幸福已经完结
冬天过去，河水上涨
我那时爱你，未来亦将这样
然而这儿已没人可以说话

The world has gone black before my eyes

The world of research has gone berserk
Too much paperwork
Albert's in the graveyard, Frankie's raising hell
I'm beginning to believe what the scriptures tell

I'm going where the Southern crosses the Yellow Dog
Get away from all these demagogues
And these bad luck women stick like glue
It's either one or the other or neither of the two

She says, "Look out daddy, don't want you to tear your pants.
You can get wrecked in this dance."
They say whiskey will kill ya, but I don't think it will
I'm riding with you to the top of the hill

Oh, I miss you Nettie Moore
And my happiness is o'er

我眼前的世界黯淡无光

研究世界发狂了
太多纸面作业
阿尔伯特在坟下，弗朗姬闹翻天 [1]
我开始相信圣典所言

我要去"南方"与"黄狗"的交会点 [2]
远离这些煽动者
这些倒霉女人就像胶水一样黏
要么是其一，要么都不是

她说："小心爸，别把裤子扯破了。
这一支舞会把你报废。"
他们说威士忌会要你的命，我不这么看
我会与你一起驰上山顶

啊，我想你妮蒂·摩尔
我的幸福已经完结

---

[1] "阿尔伯特在坟下，弗朗姬闹翻天"，美国民歌《弗朗姬与阿尔伯特》，讲述了弗朗姬因发现阿尔伯特出轨而将他枪杀的故事。
[2] "南方"指南方铁路，"黄狗"是亚祖三角洲铁路的昵称。两条铁路曾在穆尔黑德交会。据传，1903 年 W. C. 汉迪在此地听到一位老人演唱《南方与黄狗交会的地方》，后在此基础上创作了《黄狗蓝调》。汉迪后来被称颂为"蓝调之父"，"'南方'与'黄狗'的交会点"也成为蓝调的一个传奇地点。

Winter's gone, the river's on the rise

I loved you then and ever shall

But there's no one here that's left to tell

The world has gone black before my eyes

Don't know why my baby never looked so good before

I don't have to wonder no more

She been cooking all day and it's gonna take me all night

I can't eat all that stuff in a single bite

The Judge is coming in, everybody rise

Lift up your eyes

You can do what you please, you don't need my advice

Before you call me any dirty names you better think twice

Getting light outside, the temperature dropped

I think the rain has stopped

I'm going to make you come to grips with fate

When I'm through with you, you'll learn to keep your business
   straight

Oh, I miss you Nettie Moore

And my happiness is o'er

Winter's gone, the river's on the rise

I loved you then and ever shall

But there's no one here that's left to tell

冬天过去，河水上涨
我那时爱你，未来亦将这样
然而这儿已没人可以说话
我眼前的世界黯淡无光

不知为何，我的宝贝从没这么好过
我再也不用瞎琢磨
她整天在做饭而这得花去我整晚
我无法一口吃下这一餐

法官进来了，全体起立
抬起你的眼看看
你可以随便搞，无须听我建议
用脏话叫我前最好多想两遍

外面天光已亮，降温了
想必是雨已经停了
我要让你扼住命运
等我们作了了结，你将学会
　料理自己

啊，我想你妮蒂·摩尔
我的幸福已经完结
冬天过去，河水上涨
我那时爱你，未来亦将这样
然而这儿已没人可以说话

The world has gone black before my eyes

The bright spark of the steady lights
Has dimmed my sights
When you're around all my grief gives 'way
A lifetime with you is like some heavenly day

Everything I've ever known to be right has been proven wrong
I'll be drifting along
The woman I'm lovin', she rules my heart
No knife could ever cut our love apart

Today I'll stand in faith and raise
The voice of praise
The sun is strong, I'm standing in the light
I wish to God that it were night

Oh, I miss you Nettie Moore
And my happiness is o'er
Winter's gone, the river's on the rise
I loved you then and ever shall
But there's no one here that's left to tell
The world has gone black before my eyes

我眼前的世界黯淡无光

稳固的灯闪着明亮的火花
减弱了我的视力
你在我身旁我的悲伤就会一扫而去
与你共度的一生就像天堂里的日子

所有我以为对的都已证明是错的
未来的我只是随波逐流
我爱的女人，她控制了我的心
钢刀也斩不断我们的爱情

今天我将秉持信念站起
并提高我赞美的音量
日头很毒，我站在阳光里
我祈求上帝这是晚上

啊，我想你妮蒂·摩尔
我的幸福已经完结
冬天过去，河水上涨
我那时爱你，未来亦将这样
然而这儿已没人可以说话
我眼前的世界黯淡无光

THE LEVEE'S GONNA BREAK

If it keep on rainin' the levee gonna break
If it keep on rainin' the levee gonna break
Everybody saying this is a day only the Lord could make

Well I worked on the levee Mama, both night and day
Well I worked on the levee Mama, both night and day
I got to the river and I threw my clothes away

I paid my time and now I'm as good as new
I paid my time and now I'm as good as new
They can't take me back, not unless I want them to

If it keep on rainin' the levee gonna break
If it keep on rainin' the levee gonna break
Some of these people gonna strip you of all they can take

I can't stop here, I ain't ready to unload
I can't stop here, I ain't ready to unload
Riches and salvation can be waiting behind the next bend in

大堤就要决口 [1]

如果雨一直下大堤就会决口
如果雨一直下大堤就会决口
人人都说这种日子只有上主造得出

唉我在堤上干活妈妈，夜晚连着白天
唉我在堤上干活妈妈，夜晚连着白天
我到了河边，我把衣服甩一边

我付清了时间，现在我恢复如新
我付清了时间，现在我恢复如新
他们不能把我抓回去，除非我要他们这样

如果雨一直下大堤就会决口
如果雨一直下大堤就会决口
这里有些人，他们会尽其所能将你扒光

我不能停这儿，我还没准备卸货
我不能停这儿，我还没准备卸货
金钱和救赎，可能等在下一个

---

[1] 1927 年的密西西比大洪灾在蓝调歌曲中经常被唱起，比如"堪萨斯"乔·麦科伊与"孟菲斯"米妮的早期歌曲《当大堤决口》。

the road

I picked you up from the gutter and this is the thanks I get
I picked you up from the gutter and this is the thanks I get
You say you want me to quit ya, I told you no, not just yet

I look in your eyes, I see nobody else but me
I look in your eyes, I see nobody other than me
I see all that I am and all I hope to be

If it keep on rainin' the levee gonna break
If it keep on rainin' the levee gonna break
Some of these people don't know which road to take

When I'm with you I forget I was ever blue
When I'm with you I forget I was ever blue
Without you there's no meaning in anything I do

Some people on the road carrying everything that they own
Some people on the road carrying everything that they own
Some people got barely enough skin to cover their bones

Put on your cat clothes, Mama, put on your evening dress
Put on your cat clothes, Mama, put on your evening dress
A few more years of hard work then there'll be a thousand
    years of happiness

拐弯处

我从阴沟捡起你，这就是我得到的回谢
我从阴沟捡起你，这就是我得到的回谢
你说要我抛弃你，我回说不，还不到时候

我望着你的眼，除了我没看到别人
我望着你的眼，除了我没看到别的人
我看到了我的一切，以及我希望成为的一切

如果雨一直下大堤就会决口
如果雨一直下大堤就会决口
这里有些人，他们不知道选哪条路走

我和你一起时我忘了我一直忧郁
我和你一起时我忘了我一直忧郁
没有你我干什么都没意思

路上有些人带上了他们所有的家当
路上有些人带上了他们所有的家当
有些人几乎没有足够的皮包住骨头

穿上你的猫衣裳，妈妈，穿上你的晚礼服
穿上你的猫衣裳，妈妈，穿上你的晚礼服
再多几年辛苦，就会有千年的
　　幸福

If it keep on rainin' the levee gonna break
If it keep on rainin' the levee gonna break
I tried to get you to love me, but I won't repeat that mistake

If it keep on rainin' the levee gonna break
If it keep on rainin' the levee gonna break
Plenty of cheap stuff out there still around to take

I woke up this morning, butter and eggs in my bed
I woke up this morning, butter and eggs in my bed
I ain't got enough room to even raise my head

Come back, baby, say we never more will part
Come back, baby, say we never more will part
Don't be a stranger without a brain or heart

If it keep on rainin' the levee gonna break
If it keep on rainin' the levee gonna break
Some people still sleepin', some people are wide awake

如果雨一直下大堤就会决口
如果雨一直下大堤就会决口
我试过让你爱上我，但我不会一错再错

如果雨一直下大堤就会决口
如果雨一直下大堤就会决口
那儿还有许多便宜货可以拿走

今儿早上我醒来，床上是蛋和黄油
今儿早上我醒来，床上是蛋和黄油
甚至我没有足够的空间抬起头

回来吧，宝贝，说我们永不离分
回来吧，宝贝，说我们永不离分
别再做无脑无心的陌路人

如果雨一直下大堤就会决口
如果雨一直下大堤就会决口
有些人还在睡，有些人完全醒了

AIN'T TALKIN'

As I walked out tonight in the mystic garden
The wounded flowers were dangling from the vines
I was passing by yon cool and crystal fountain
Someone hit me from behind

Ain't talkin', just walkin'
Through this weary world of woe
Heart burnin', still yearnin'
No one on earth would ever know

They say prayer has the power to help
So pray for me mother
In the human heart an evil spirit can dwell
I'm trying to love my neighbor and do good unto others
But oh, mother, things ain't going well

Ain't talkin', just walkin'
I'll burn that bridge before you can cross
Heart burnin', still yearnin'
They'll be no mercy for you once you've lost

Now I'm all worn down by weepin'

不作声

今晚我退席走入那神秘花园
残花在藤蔓上倒垂
我路过清冷的水晶喷泉
有人从身后撞我

不作声，惟前行
穿过这疲惫的悲凉人世
心燃着，仍怀憧憬
这世上终无人可知

人说祈祷大有功效
所以母亲，请为我祷告
人心会住进恶魔的灵
我一直努力爱邻舍，善待他人
但是啊母亲，事情并非一帆风顺

不作声，惟前行
你过河前我会把桥烧毁
心燃着，仍怀憧憬
一旦你输了，他们不会怜悯

现在我被哭泣折磨

My eyes are filled with tears, my lips are dry
If I catch my opponents ever sleepin'
I'll just slaughter them where they lie

Ain't talkin', just walkin'
Through a world mysterious and vague
Heart burnin', still yearnin'
Walking through the cities of the plague

The whole world is filled with speculation
The whole wide world which people say is round
They will tear your mind away from contemplation
They will jump on your misfortune when you're down

Ain't talkin', just walkin'
Eatin' hog-eyed grease in hog-eyed town
Heart burnin', still yearnin'
Someday you'll be glad to have me around

They will crush you with wealth and power
Every waking moment you could crack
I'll make the most of one last extra hour
I'll avenge my father's death then I'll step back

Ain't talkin', just walkin'
Hand me down my walkin' cane

眼里都是泪，嘴唇也干了
如果撞上对手正在酣睡
我会宰掉他们，就在其栖身之地

不作声，惟前行
穿过诡秘暧昧的世界
心燃着，仍怀憧憬
走过一座座瘟疫之城

整个世界充满了猜疑
这广大世界人们说它是圆的
他们将把你的心从沉思中拖走
他们会对你落井下石

不作声，惟前行
在猪眼镇饱食猪眼油脂
心燃着，仍怀憧憬
有天你会因为有我而欢欣

他们将用钱权碾压
每次梦醒你都可能崩溃
我会充分利用最后的一小时
我将报杀父之仇然后告退

不作声，惟前行
麻烦把拐杖递我

Heart burnin', still yearnin'
Got to get you out of my miserable brain

It's bright in the heavens and the wheels are flying
Fame and honor never seem to fade
The fire's gone out but the light is never dying
Who says I can't get heavenly aid?

Ain't talkin', just walkin'
Carrying a dead man's shield
Heart burnin', still yearnin'
Walkin' with a toothache in my heel

The suffering is unending
Every nook and cranny has its tears
I'm not playing, I'm not pretending
I'm not nursing any superfluous fears

Ain't talkin', just walkin'
Walkin' ever since the other night
Heart burnin', still yearnin'
Walkin' 'til I'm clean out of sight

As I walked out in the mystic garden
On a hot summer day, hot summer lawn
Excuse me, ma'am, I beg your pardon

心燃着，仍怀憧憬
我要把你赶出我悲惨的头颅

乾坤朗朗，巨轮飞转
名望和荣耀似乎永不褪色
火焰熄灭，但光芒永驻
谁说我得不到上苍的眷顾？

不作声，惟前行
身负一面死人的盾
心燃着，仍怀憧憬
忍着脚后跟的牙疼前进

苦难无休止
每个角落缝隙都有它的泪水
我没在演，我不是装
我并非在养育多余的恐惧

不作声，惟前行
从那一夜走到今天
心燃着，仍怀憧憬
直走到无人能见

当我退席走入那神秘花园
在炎炎夏日，炎炎夏日的草地
原谅我夫人，我请求您宽恕

There's no one here, the gardener is gone

Ain't talkin', just walkin'
Up the road around the bend
Heart burnin', still yearnin'
In the last outback, at the world's end

这儿空无一人，园丁也已离去

不作声，惟前行
沿路拐过那道弧线
心燃着，仍怀憧憬
在最后的内陆，在世界的终点

CAN'T ESCAPE FROM YOU

Oh the evening train is rolling

All along the homeward way

All my hopes are over the horizon

All my dreams have gone astray

The hillside darkly shaded

Stars fall from above

All the joys of earth have faded

The nights untouched by love

I'll be here 'til tomorrow

Beneath a shroud of gray

I'll pretend I'm free from sorrow

My heart is miles away

The dead bells are ringing

My train is overdue

To your memory I'm clinging

I can't escape from you

Well I hear the sound of thunder

Roaring loud and long

Sometimes you've got to wonder

God knows I've done no wrong

You've wasted all your power

无法逃离你

啊傍晚列车滚滚向前
朝着那回家的路
我全部的希望都在地平线那边
我全部的梦都已迷途
山坡蒙上阴影
群星从天而降
尘世欢愉俱已消隐
这夜再不为爱所动
我会待这儿直到明天
盖着这灰白的裹尸布
我会装作自己不再伤感
我的心远在他处
死亡钟声敲响了
我的火车晚点了
紧依着对你的回忆
我无法逃离你

嗯我听见雷鸣
隆隆巨响连绵不绝
有时你不得不疑心
上帝知道我并未做错
你已浪费所有气力

You threw out the Christmas pie

You'll wither like a flower

And play the fool and die

I'm neither sad nor sorry

I'm all dressed up in black

I fought for fame and glory

You tried to break my back

In the far off sweet forever

The sunshine breaking through

We should have walked together

I can't escape from you

I cannot grasp the shadows

That gather near the door

Rain fall 'round my window

I wish I'd seen you more

The path is ever winding

The stars they never age

The morning light is blinding

All the world's a stage

Should be the time of gladness

Happy faces everywhere

But the mystery of madness

Is propagating in the air

I don't like the city

Not like some folks do

你丢弃了圣诞派
你会像花一样枯萎
出尽洋相然后死去
我不难过也不遗憾
从上到下一身黑衣
我为名誉和荣耀而战
你却想打断我的脊骨
那遥远的永恒甜蜜之地
阳光穿透了云层
我们本该走到一起
我无法逃离你

我抓不住那些影子
它们在门前聚集
雨落在窗子四周
我还是想见你
路总是弯弯曲曲
星辰永不衰败
晨光令人盲目
全世界是个舞台
这本该是欢愉时分
到处是幸福的脸
但是那疯狂的秘密
正在空气中扩散
我不喜欢这个城市
不像有些人

Isn't it a pity

I can't escape from you?

这岂不是可惜
我无法逃离你?

HUCK'S TUNE

Well I wandered alone
Through a desert of stone
And I dreamt of my future wife
My sword's in my hand
And I'm next in command
In this version of death called life
My plate and my cup
Are right straight up
I took a rose from the hand of a child
When I kiss your lips
The honey drips
But I'm gonna have to put you down for a while

Every day we meet
On any old street
And you're in your girlish prime
The short and the tall
Are coming to the ball
I go there all the time

赫克之歌 [1]

哦我独自一人

流浪穿过戈壁

梦见我未来的妻

我手里仗着剑

我是下一任指挥官

在这版叫生活的死亡里

我的盘子我的茶杯

都立得笔直

从小童手里我拿过一枝玫瑰

我亲吻你的嘴

蜜汁滴落

但是我不得不将你放下一会儿

我们每天都碰面

在随便哪条老街上

正值你豆蔻初开的时光

矮个子和高个子

都来参加舞会

每次我都到场

---

[1]　这是为电影《幸运赌神》（*Lucky You*, 2007）所作的歌曲，赫克是
片中男主角，一位牌技高超的赌徒。

Behind every tree

There's something to see

The river is wider than a mile

I tried you twice

You couldn't be nice

I'm gonna have to put you down for a while

Here come the nurse

With money in her purse

Here come the ladies and men

You push it all in

And you've no chance to win

You play 'em on down to the end

I'm laying in the sand

Getting a sunshine tan

Moving along, riding in style

From my toes to my head

You knock me dead

I'm gonna have to put you down for a while

I count the years

And I shed no tears

I'm blinded to what might have been

Nature's voice

Makes my heart rejoice

Play me the wild song of the wind

每棵树的后面
总会发现什么
这条河足有一英里多宽
我试探了你两回
你都不来电
我不得不将你放下一会儿

那护士来了
钱包里装着钱
女士们先生们来了
你押上了全部
但是你没机会赢
你一直搏到最终
我躺在沙滩上
皮肤晒成小麦色
招摇过市，座驾入时
从头到脚
你把我迷倒
我不得不将你放下一会儿

我数着年头
一滴泪没流
看不见本已发生的一切
大自然的声音
令我心雀跃
为我奏一曲狂野大风歌

I found hopeless love

In the room above

When the sun and the weather were mild

You're as fine as wine

I ain't handing you no line

But I'm gonna have to put you down for a while

All the merry little elves

Can go hang themselves

My faith is as cold as can be

I'm stacked high to the roof

And I'm not without proof

If you don't believe me, come see

You think I'm blue

I think so too

In my words, you'll find no guile

The game's gotten old

The deck's gone cold

And I'm gonna have to put you down for a while

The game's gotten old

The deck's gone cold

I'm gonna have to put you down for a while

我找到了无望的爱
在楼上房间
此时风和日丽
你美得就像酒
我不是跟你套瓷
但是我不得不将你放下一会儿

所有的快乐小精灵
都可以自行了断了
我的信念已变冷酷
我的钱堆到了屋顶
我不是空口无凭
不信你来见识见识
你觉得我忧郁
我也这么以为
用我的话说，你看不出有问题
这游戏已玩旧
纸牌已经凉透
而我不得不将你放下一会儿

这游戏已玩旧
纸牌已经凉透
我不得不将你放下一会儿

TEMPEST
暴风雨

6. Set 'im up Joe, play Walkin' the Floor
It's not like nobody's ever asked you before
~~the~~ cheek the liquor and you write Amens
while the smile of Heaven descends
If love is a sin, then beauty's a crime
All things are beautiful in their time
The black & white, the yellow and brown
It's all right here for you in Scarlet Town

                They tell me that
            The Law is the Law

— Ying/my I give   — the ... on
  away the bells   won't be friend-
  gave yourself   ed rude

                    Some fentaluys
                    crossed the
                    line
                    protect the quality
                    protect   \ I expect
                    the   school boy prays

The doors are chained

2012 年，鲍勃·迪伦 71 岁。他的"永不停止的巡演"还在路上，已经持续 24 年了。推出上一张全原创录音室专辑，是 3 年前的事。同年，他推出了人生中第一张圣诞歌曲专辑《心中的圣诞节》(*Christmas in the Heart*)，这也是他第 34 张录音室专辑。他出生于犹太人家庭，小时候从不过圣诞节。

　　2012 年 9 月 11 日，《暴风雨》由哥伦比亚唱片公司发行，是迪伦第 35 张录音室专辑。他的创作力并未衰竭，似乎还增强了。不同于年轻时的那种爆发，一年可以出 2 张专辑，现在他的动作缓慢，但是力量雄浑。

　　"暴风雨"意指英语世界一代代流传、可能还将传说下去的"泰坦尼克号"沉船事件。发生于百余年前的这场人类历史上最大的海难，吞噬掉 1600 多条生命。迪伦以这 3 个字为题，写成一首有 45 段歌词，足足要唱 13 分54 秒，却只用了 3 个和弦的歌。死亡、死亡、死亡，反复、反复、反复，但整首歌听上去并无重复沉闷之感。它附带证明：歌曲最重要的是歌词。一首好词，哪怕只是念诵，也足以动人、绝对成立。而迪伦，正是这方面的大师。

　　但"暴风雨"又不仅指那场海难。在这个单词前面，迪伦没有加定冠词。这或许意味着，这不是某一场暴风雨，而是所有的暴风雨，是人类所有的劫难、所有的终篇。

专辑通篇充斥了死亡。只说死亡，或失之偏颇，还必须提及它的另一面，即黑暗歌词另一面的光：这是安魂曲，迪伦所能布置的最庄严、最盛大、最伟岸的安魂曲。

专辑中有一首歌《锡天使》，给我留下了更强烈的印象。在一个看似不可解的三角恋困局中——我没想到迪伦是这样决绝——所有生命都以惨烈的方式终结。但这终结却不是归零和寂灭，生命终结的同时，有一种比生命更重要的东西站立起来，极其强悍和确定。

《前进约翰》受到普遍的关注，作为终曲的终曲，它是一个强音，而非陷于沉痛。想想吧，一个已经故去的人，还怎么前进？但迪伦唱的就是前进。这就像是以前他说的，"死亡不是终结"，这首歌是以铿锵的进行曲，雄辩地演示给你看：死亡不是终结。

作为叙事诗/叙事曲的一次大丰收，这张专辑是多彩的：没有任何作品文体重复，也没有任何歌曲题材相似。作者脸上的表情、心里的思虑、眼光中的幻影，也都不一样——阴晴不定、忽明忽灭，是生命结晶、民间神话和历史棱镜的多向折射。专辑中的这些歌曲彼此交织、相互支持，共有着黑色抒情的死之光芒，形成史诗般的宏伟。每首歌曲都承载着多重记忆的重压，带着一个伟大世界、一个光怪陆离的时代正迅速从我们指缝溜走的暗示。

《迪尤肯汽笛》是只有在老年才能写出的歌曲，它穿过了童年，剖开了一生，搏动起一颗装载着古怪老美国的大心脏。

《午夜刚过》充满了神秘和杀气，他是要杀人，还是要爱一个人至死？

《窄路》在说美国这个国家的不堪，也在讲自己这一生无能。《蹉跎岁月》讲彼此相伴的两人，不过是像两列相隔40英里的火车并排疾驰，将这一生报废。

《以血偿付》讲复仇，一个都不饶恕，并暗指基督不用自我牺牲。《猩红镇》是比《窄路》更明确的关于美国的隐喻，辉煌到极致却也大限将至。《古罗马王》属于那种逗死人的幽默，黑帮形迹仿佛最严肃的国事，内讧和覆灭仿佛古罗马的陷落。

而这位老人的声音，愈加沧桑和黑暗。他沉浸在传统中，谈起这一生旧事，态度绝无宽谅，而呈现为一种耿耿于怀。虽然他的语气有时温柔，有时顽皮，但始终有令人惊心的残酷，甚至在他无与伦比地激起人们的振奋之时。

音乐批评家威尔·赫米斯（Will Hermes）充满洞察力地指出，迪伦的一生母题，尤其是最后3张专辑——"基于传统形式并借鉴了永恒的主题：爱、斗争、死亡"。

赫米斯说："在歌词方面，迪伦依然处于他的巅峰。他到处开玩笑，随时掉书袋，抛洒避开了肤浅的文字游戏和寓言，并像一个着火的即兴说唱歌手一样引用别人的话。"

迪伦依然超乎想象，令人惊叹。2012年1月至3月，在加州圣莫尼卡，巡演乐队准确而招摇地为迪伦的"古老歌曲"注入了当代能量，以现场方式录制了这张专辑。

DUQUESNE WHISTLE
(WITH ROBERT HUNTER)

Listen to that Duquesne whistle blowin'
Blowin' like it's gonna sweep my world away
I'm gonna stop in Carbondale and keep on going
That Duquesne train gonna ride me night and day

You say I'm a gambler, you say I'm a pimp
But I ain't neither one

Listen to that Duquesne whistle blowin'
Sound like it's on a final run

Listen to that Duquesne whistle blowin'
Blowin' like she never blowed before
Blue light blinkin', red light glowin'
Blowin' like she's at my chamber door

You smiling through the fence at me
Just like you always smiled before

迪尤肯[1] 汽笛
（与罗伯特·亨特合作）

听那迪尤肯汽笛长鸣
那长鸣像是要卷走我的世界
我会在卡本代尔[2] 经停，然后继续前行
迪尤肯火车载着我日日夜夜

你说我赌棍，你说我皮条客
其实我两个都不是

听那迪尤肯汽笛长鸣
听起来就像是它最后的旅程

听那迪尤肯汽笛长鸣
就像是她以前从未出声
蓝灯闪烁，红灯幽幽
那长鸣像是她来到我门口

你隔着栅栏对我笑
恰似从前，你总是这样笑

---

[1] 迪尤肯，宾夕法尼亚列车旧称，目前仍在运行，从纽约到匹兹堡。
[2] 卡本代尔，铁路枢纽城市，美国南北向与东西向铁路的交会点。

Listen to that Duquesne whistle blowin'
Blowin' like she ain't gonna blow no more

Can't you hear that Duquesne whistle blowin'
Blowin' like the sky's gonna blow apart
You're the only thing alive that keeps me goin'
You're like a time bomb in my heart

I can hear a sweet voice gently calling
Must be the Mother of our Lord

Listen to that Duquesne whistle blowin'
Blowin' like my woman's on board

Listen to that Duquesne whistle blowin'
Blowin' like it's gonna blow my blues away
You ole rascal, I know exactly where you're goin'
I'll lead you there myself at the break of day

I wake up every morning with that woman in my bed
Everybody telling me she's gone to my head

Listen to that Duquesne whistle blowin'
Blowin' like it's gonna kill me dead

听那迪尤肯汽笛长鸣
那长鸣像是她再也不出声

你听不到迪尤肯汽笛的长鸣吗
那长鸣像是天空就要炸裂成两半
你是唯一驱使我前行的活物
你就像是埋在我心中的定时炸弹

我能听见一个甜美的声音在轻呼
那一定是我们的上主之母

听那迪尤肯汽笛长鸣
那长鸣像是我的女人上了车

听那迪尤肯汽笛长鸣
那长鸣就像是要带走我的忧郁
你这老流氓，我很清楚你去哪
天一亮我就会带你去

每天早晨醒来那个女人都在床上
人人说，她已经钻入我心房

听那迪尤肯汽笛长鸣
那长鸣就像是要杀了我一样

Can't you hear that Duquesne whistle blowin'
Blowin' through another no-good town
The lights of my native land are glowin'
I wonder if they'll know me next time around

I wonder if that old oak tree's still standing
That old oak tree, the one we used to climb

Listen to that Duquesne whistle blowin'
Blowin' like she's blowin' right on time

你听不到迪尤肯汽笛的长鸣吗
那长鸣穿过又一个无用的城镇
我故乡的灯火还在闪烁
不知道下次回来它认不认得我

不知道那老橡树是否还在
那棵老橡树哦，就是以前我们常爬的那棵

听那迪尤肯汽笛长鸣
恰似她准时吹奏的声音

SOON AFTER MIDNIGHT

I'm searching for phrases to sing your praises
I need to tell someone
It's soon after midnight and my day has just begun

A gal named Honey took my money
She was passing by
It's soon after midnight and the moon is in my eye

My heart is cheerful, it's never fearful
I been down on the killing floors
I'm in no great hurry, I'm not afraid of your fury
I've faced stronger walls than yours

Charlotte's a harlot, dresses in scarlet
Mary dresses in green
It's soon after midnight and I've got a date with a fairy queen

They chirp and they chatter, what does it matter
They're lying there dying in their blood
Two Timing Slim, who's ever heard of him?
I'll drag his corpse through the mud

午夜刚过

我搜寻着颂扬你的词句
我必须对人说
午夜刚过，我的一天刚刚开始

一个叫"心肝"的妞拿走我的钱
擦身而去
午夜刚过，我的眼中有明月

我心怡然，从不畏惧
我一直都在屠宰场里
我从容不迫，不惧你的狂暴
我面对过比你更强大的城堡

夏洛特这荡妇，一袭猩红
玛丽身着绿衣
午夜刚过，我和仙后有约

他们叽叽喳喳又喋喋不休，那又怎样呢
他们躺在那儿，在血泊中奄奄一息
脚踩两只船的老油条，谁听说过他？
我要拖他的尸首过泥水

It's now or never, more than ever

When I met you I didn't think you would do

It's soon after midnight and I don't want nobody but you

现在机不可失，更胜于任何时候
遇见你时，我未料你会如此
午夜刚过，我谁都不要只要你

NARROW WAY

I'm gonna walk across the desert 'til I'm in my right mind
I won't even think about what I left behind
Nothin' back there anyway I can call my own
Go back home, leave me alone

It's a long road, it's a long and narrow way
If I can't work up to you
You'll have to work down to me someday

Ever since the British burned the white house down
There's a bleeding wound in the heart of town
I saw you drinking from an empty cup
I saw you buried and I saw you dug up

It's a long road, it's a long and narrow way
If I can't work up to you
You'll have to work down to me someday

Look down angel, from the skies
Help my weary soul to rise
I kissed your cheek, I dragged your plow
You broke my heart, I was your friend 'til now

窄路

我要走过沙漠直到头脑清醒
以致不用想自己会留下什么
反正后面也没啥属于我
回家吧，别管我

这是一段长旅，一条长长窄路
如果我跟不上
总有一天你会放缓让我靠近

自从英国人烧掉了白宫
市中心便有一道流血伤痕
我见你从空杯啜饮
我见你被埋葬，又见你被人挖出

这是一段长旅，一条长长窄路
如果我跟不上
总有一天你会放缓让我靠近

看下面啊天使，从天空望下去
请助我疲惫的灵魂上升
我吻你的颊，我拉你的犁
你伤我的心，此前我们一直是朋友

It's a long road, it's a long and narrow way
If I can't work up to you
You'll have to work down to me someday

In the courtyard of the golden sun
You stand and fight or you break and run
You went and lost your lovely head
For a drink of wine and a crust of bread

It's a long road, it's a long and narrow way
If I can't work up to you
You'll have to work down to me someday

We looted and we plundered on distant shores
Why is my share not equal to yours?
Your father left you, your mother too
Even death has washed his hands of you

It's a long road, it's a long and narrow way
If I can't work up to you
You'll have to work down to me someday

This is hard country to stay alive in
Blades are everywhere and they're breaking my skin
I'm armed to the hilt and I'm struggling hard

这是一段长旅，一条长长窄路
如果我跟不上
总有一天你会放缓让我靠近

在这金色阳光的庭院
你要么挺身战斗，要么转身逃离
你走了，弄丢了你可爱的头
为了一杯酒和一片面包皮

这是一段长旅，一条长长窄路
如果我跟不上
总有一天你会放缓让我靠近

我们在遥远的海岸疯狂劫掠
为什么我那一份不与你的一样多？
你父亲离开你，你母亲离开你
就连死神也对你不顾不管

这是一段长旅，一条长长窄路
如果我跟不上
总有一天你会放缓让我靠近

这是个让人活不下去的国度
遍地是刀丛，割开我的肌肤
我全副武装，苦苦挣扎

You won't get out of here unscarred

It's a long road, it's a long and narrow way
If I can't work up to you
You'll have to work down to me someday

You got too many lovers waiting at the wall
If I had a thousand tongues I couldn't count them all
Yesterday I could have thrown them all in the sea
Today, even one may be too much for me

It's a long road, it's a long and narrow way
If I can't work up to you
You'll have to work down to me someday

Cake walking baby, you can do no wrong
Put your arms around me where they belong
I want to take you on a roller coaster ride
Lay my hands all over you, tie you to my side

It's a long road, it's a long and narrow way
If I can't work up to you
You'll have to work down to me someday

I got a heavy stacked woman with a smile on her face
And she has crowned my soul with grace

你无法毫发无伤退出

这是一段长旅，一条长长窄路
如果我跟不上
总有一天你会放缓让我靠近

你有太多情人等在大墙下
我纵有一千根舌头也数不清
昨天我本可以将他们都扔进海
今天，就算是一个我可能都扔不动

这是一段长旅，一条长长窄路
如果我跟不上
总有一天你会放缓让我靠近

走蛋糕步的宝贝儿，你可以不出错
把你的双臂搂着我啊，它们本该这样
我要带你坐过山车
双手把你整个抱住，把你绑在我身旁

这是一段长旅，一条长长窄路
如果我跟不上
总有一天你会放缓让我靠近

我找了个笑盈盈的丰腴女人
她以优雅冠冕了我的灵魂

I'm still hurting from an arrow that pierced my chest
I'm gonna have to take my head and bury it
    between your breasts

It's a long road, it's a long and narrow way
If I can't work up to you
You'll have to work down to me someday

Been dark all night, but now it's dawn
The moving finger is moving on
You can guard me while I sleep
Kiss away the tears I weep

It's a long road, it's a long and narrow way
If I can't work up to you
You'll have to work down to me someday

I love women and she loves men
We've been to the West and we going back again
I heard a voice at the dusk of day
Saying, "Be gentle brother, be gentle and pray"

It's a long road, it's a long and narrow way
If I can't work up to you
You'll have to work down to me someday

那支刺穿我胸膛的箭仍在使我痛苦
我得把头深埋进
　你的胸脯

这是一段长旅，一条长长窄路
如果我跟不上
总有一天你会放缓让我靠近

彻夜黑暗，但现在已是黎明
移动的手指还在移动
等我睡去你会保护我
吻去我流出的泪水

这是一段长旅，一条长长窄路
如果我跟不上
总有一天你会放缓让我靠近

我爱女人，她爱男人
我们去了西部，然后我们又折回
黄昏时我听见有个声音
说"轻点儿兄弟，请轻点儿祷告"

这是一段长旅，一条长长窄路
如果我跟不上
总有一天你会放缓让我靠近

LONG AND WASTED YEARS

It's been such a long, long time
Since we loved each other and our hearts were true
One time, for one brief day
I was the man for you

Last night I heard you talking in your sleep
Saying things you shouldn't say
Oh, baby
You just might have to go to jail some day

Is there a place we can go?
Is there anybody we can see?
Maybe what's right for you
Isn't really right for me

I ain't seen my family in twenty years
That ain't easy to understand
They may be dead by now
I lost track of them after they lost their land

Shake it up baby, twist and shout
You tell me what it's all about

蹉跎岁月

时光已过去太久太久
自从我们相爱，满怀真情
有过一次，短暂的一天
我是你的男人

昨夜我听见你在梦中呓语
说了些你不该说的事
哦，宝贝儿
有一天你可能会进监狱

我们可有地方去？
我们可有什么人要见？
也许适合你的
真的不适合我

我已有二十年没见家人了
这事儿不容易理解
他们可能已经不在了
他们失去土地后，我们就断了联系

赶紧醒醒宝贝，扭动并喊叫
告诉我这都是怎么了

What you doing out in the sun anyway?
Don't you know the sun can burn your brains right out?

My enemy slammed into the earth
I don't know what he was worth
But he lost it all, everything and more
What a blithering fool he took me for

I wear dark glasses to cover my eyes
There're secrets in them I can't disguise
Come back, baby
If I hurt your feelings, I apologize

Two trains running side by side
Forty miles wide down the Eastern line
You don't have to go, I just came to you
Because you're a friend of mine

I think when my back was turned
The whole world behind me burned
Maybe today, if not today, maybe tomorrow
Maybe there'll be a limit on all my sorrow

We cried on a cold and frosty morn'
We cried because our souls were torn
So much for tears
So much for those long and wasted years

你在太阳底下要干吗？
不知道太阳会烧坏你脑子吗？

我的敌人一头栽倒在地
不知道他值几个钱
但他失去了一切，甚至比一切更多
他把我当成十足的笨蛋

我用墨镜遮住眼
里面有我无法遮掩的秘密
回来吧，宝贝儿
如果我伤了你的情，我深表歉意

两列火车并排疾驰
沿着东线相隔四十英里
你不必走，我只是来找你而已
因为你是我的朋友

我想只要我背转身
身后的世界就会化为灰烬
也许今天，若非今天可能是明天
我的悲伤就会抵达极限

我们在寒冷而结霜的早晨哭泣
我们因为灵魂被撕裂而哭泣
眼泪就到此为止
蹉跎岁月就到此为止

PAY IN BLOOD

Well I'm grinding my life away, steady and sure
Nothing more wretched than what I must endure
I'm drenched in the light that shines from the sun
I could stone you to death for the wrongs that you done

Sooner or later you'll make a mistake
I'll put you in a chain that you never can break
Legs and arms and body and bone
I pay in blood, but not my own

Night after night, day after day
They strip your useless hopes away
The more I take, the more I give
The more I die, the more I live

I got something in my pocket make your eyeballs swim
I got dogs that could tear you limb to limb
I'm circling around in the southern zone
I pay in blood, but not my own

Another politician pumping out his piss
Another ragged beggar blowin' ya a kiss

以血偿付

哦一点点将生命磨碎，踏实而明确
世间万物都没我要忍受的事恶劣
我浸泡在太阳放射的光辉里
为你犯的错我会用石头砸死你

迟早你会犯错
我将给你戴上挣不脱的枷锁
腿和胳膊和身体和骨头
我以血偿付，但不用我自己的血

一夜又一夜，一天又一天
时间剥下你百无一用的期盼
我得的越多，给的就越多
我死的越多，活的也就越多

我口袋里有样东西，让你的眼珠打转
我养了一群狗，能把你撕成碎片
我在南区兜圈子
我以血偿付，但不用我自己的血

又一个政客撒尿
又一个叫花子抛来飞吻

Life is short and it don't last long

They'll hang you in the morning and sing ya a song

Someone must have slipped a drug in your wine

You gulped it down and you lost your mind

My head so hard, it must be made of stone

I pay in blood, but not my own

How I made it back home nobody knows

Or how I survived so many blows

I been through hell, what good did it do?

My conscience is clear, what about you?

I'll give you justice, I'll fatten your purse

Show me your moral virtues first

Hear me holler, hear me moan

I pay in blood but not my own

You bit your lover in the bed

Come here I'll break your lousy head

Our nation must be saved and freed

You been accused of murder, how do you plead?

This is how I spend my days

人生短促，不可长久
他们会在早晨吊死你，再为你唱首歌

一定有人在酒里下了药
你一饮而尽，然后就失去理智
我的头好硬，一定是石头做的
我以血偿付，但不用我自己的血

没人知道我是怎么到家的
没人知道我经受这么多打击怎么还活着
我到地狱走了一遭，这有何用？
我问心无愧，那么你呢？

我会给你公道，我会喂肥你的钱包
先让我看看你那副德操
来听我呼喊，听我呜咽
我以血偿付，但不用我自己的血

你在床上咬你的情人
过这儿来，看我不打烂你的狗头
我们的国家必须拯救并得到自由
你被指控谋杀，你如何辩护？

我就是这么过来的

I came to bury not to praise

I'll drink my fill and sleep alone

I pay in blood, but not my own

我来是为埋葬而不是唱赞歌 [1]

我会喝得尽兴然后独自睡去

我以血偿付，但不用我自己的血

---

[1] "我来是为埋葬而不是唱赞歌"，莎士比亚戏剧《裘力斯·凯撒》第三幕第二场："我是来埋葬凯撒，不是来赞美他。"（朱生豪译）

SCARLET TOWN

In Scarlet Town where I was born
There's ivy leaf and silver thorn
The streets have names you can't pronounce
Gold is down to a quarter of an ounce

The music starts and the people sway
Everybody says, are you going my way?
Uncle Tom still working for Uncle Bill
Scarlet Town is under the hill

Scarlet Town in the month of May
Sweet William on his deathbed lay
Mistress Mary by the side of the bed
Kissing his face, heaping prayers on his head

So brave, so true, so gentle is he
I'll weep for him as he'd weep for me
Little Boy Blue come blow your horn
In Scarlet Town where I was born

猩红镇

在猩红镇，我的出生地
有常春藤叶和银色荆棘
街道取了你念不出的名儿
黄金剩下四分之一盎司 [1]

音乐响起，人们随之起舞
每人都在问，你是不是与我同路？
汤姆叔叔仍在为比尔叔叔扛活儿
猩红镇在那山脚下

五月的猩红镇
可人儿威廉躺在床上等死
情人玛丽在床边
吻他的脸，在他头上堆上祈祷词

他那么勇，那么真，那么温雅啊
我会为他哭泣，一如他会为我哭泣
"小男孩布鲁"，来吹响你的号角
在猩红镇，我的出生地

---

[1]　1 盎司约合 28.350 克。——编者注

Scarlet Town in the hot noon hours

There's palm leaf shadows and scattered flowers

Beggars crouching at the gate

Help comes but it comes too late

On marble slabs and in fields of stone

You make your humble wishes known

I touched the garment but the hem was torn

In Scarlet Town where I was born

In Scarlet Town the end is near

The seven wonders of the world are here

The evil and the good living side by side

All human forms seem glorified

Put your heart on a platter and see who'll bite

See who'll hold you and kiss you good night

There's walnut groves and maple wood

In Scarlet Town crying won't do you no good

In Scarlet Town you fight your father's foes

Up on the hill a chilly wind blows

You fight 'em on high and you fight 'em down in

You fight 'em with whisky, morphine and gin

You got legs that can drive men mad

炽热正午的猩红镇

有棕榈叶影和四散的花

乞丐蜷缩在门前

救助来了，但实在太迟

在大理石上，在石头阵里

你让你卑微的心愿为世人所知

我摸摸衣服，可边角已破

在猩红镇，我的出生地

猩红镇大限将近

世界七大奇迹尽在此间

恶人善人比邻而居

所有人形似乎都被颂赞

把你的心放盘子里，看看谁会咬

看看谁会拥抱，吻你道晚安

这里有胡桃园和枫树林

在猩红镇哭泣没用

在猩红镇你与父亲的仇人作战

山冈上寒风凛凛

你和他们在高处拼，和他们在低处拼

和他们用威士忌、吗啡和杜松子酒拼

你的大腿能让男人发疯

A lot of things we didn't do that I wish we had
In Scarlet Town the sky is clear
You'll wish to God that you stayed right here

Set 'em up Joe, play Walking The Floor
Play it for my flat chested junkie whore
I'm staying up late and I'm making amends
While the smile of heaven descends

If love is a sin then beauty is a crime
All things are beautiful in their time
The black and the white, the yellow and the brown
It's all right there for ya in Scarlet Town

太多事都没做，真希望我们做了
猩红镇天空明净
你会祈求上帝你就留在这里

收拾停当乔，弹一曲《踱来踱去》
这一曲献给我平胸的毒虫婊子
我将熬夜做出补救
当天堂的笑突然降临

如果爱是罪孽，那美就是罪行
万物正当其时的时候都分外美丽
黑人和白人，黄种人和棕色人
全部都在猩红镇等你

EARLY ROMAN KINGS

All the early Roman Kings in their sharkskin suits
Bowties and buttons, high top boots
Driving the spikes in, blazing the rails
Nailed in their coffins in top hats and tails
Fly away little bird, fly away, flap your wings
Fly by night like the early Roman Kings

All the early Roman Kings in the early, early morn'
Coming down the mountain, distributing the corn
Speeding through the forest, racing down the track
You try to get away, they drag you back
Tomorrow is Friday, we'll see what it brings
Everybody's talking 'bout the early Roman Kings

They're peddlers and they're meddlers, they buy and they sell
They destroyed your city, they'll destroy you as well
They're lecherous and treacherous, hell bent for leather
Each of them bigger than all men put together
Sluggers and muggers wearing fancy gold rings
All the women going crazy for the early Roman Kings

古罗马王 [1]

所有的古罗马王，一身鲨鱼皮正装
领结和纽扣，高筒靴子
将钉子钉入，开辟铁路
钉入棺材，身上是大礼帽和燕尾服
飞走吧小鸟，飞走，扑打翅膀
趁着夜色高飞就像古罗马王

所有的古罗马王，一大清早
下山，分发玉米
飞速穿过森林，越过道轨
你想溜走，他们将你拖回
明天就是礼拜五，我们会看到后果
人人都在谈论古罗马王

他们是贩夫走卒，他们四处插手，买进卖出
摧毁你的城，也将摧毁你
他们好色又背信弃义，不择手段抢夺皮革
个个都比加起来更强
戴着花哨金戒指的强盗和抢匪
所有的女人都为古罗马王疯狂

---

[1] 古罗马王，20世纪六七十年代美国纽约一个帮派组织。

I'll dress up your wounds with a blood clotted rag
I ain't afraid to make love to a bitch or a hag
If you see me coming and you're standing there
Wave your handkerchief in the air
I ain't dead yet, my bell still rings
I keep my fingers crossed like the early Roman Kings

I'll strip you of life, strip you of breath
Ship you down to the house of death
One day you will ask for me
There'll be no one else that you'll want to see
Bring down my fiddle, tune up my strings
Gonna break it wide open like the early Roman Kings

I was up on black mountain the day Detroit fell
They killed them all off and they sent them to hell
Ding Dong Daddy, you're coming up short
Gonna put you on trial in a Sicilian court
I've had my fun, I've had my flings
Gonna shake 'em all down like the early Roman Kings

我会用血迹斑斑的破布装饰你的伤
我不怕和母狗与母夜叉做爱
如果你见我过来，你就站那儿
在空中挥挥手绢儿
我还没死，我的钟还在鸣响
我十指交叉就像古罗马王

我会取你性命，取你的呼吸
驾船送你去太平间
有一天你会来求我
除了我你谁都不见
把我的提琴拿过来，调好弦
我要大弹特弹就像古罗马王

我在黑山那天底特律陷落了
他们杀光了所有人，把他们都打入地狱
叮咚老爹，你棋差一招
将被送往西西里法庭受审
我快活过了，风流过了
会把他们都清理掉就像古罗马王

TIN ANGEL

It was late last night when the boss came home
To a deserted mansion and a desolate throne
Servant said, "Boss, the lady's gone
She left this morning just 'fore dawn."

"You got something to tell me, tell it to me, man.
Come to the point as straight as you can."
"Old Henry Lee, chief of the clan,
Came riding through the woods and took her by the hand."

The boss he laid back flat on his bed
He cursed the heat and he clutched his head
He pondered the future of his fate
To wait another day would be far too late

"Go fetch me my coat and my tie
And the cheapest labor that money can buy
Saddle me up my buckskin mare
If you see me go by, put up a prayer."

Well, they rode all night and they rode all day
Eastward long on the broad highway

锡天使

昨晚主人到家时天已经很晚了
他回到他荒寂的宅邸和荒凉的王座
仆人说："主人，夫人走了
今早天没亮就走了。"

"你有话要告诉我，说吧，伙计。
开门见山只管说。"
"老亨利·李，部落首领，
骑马穿林而来，牵手带走她。"

主人摊平了躺在床上
他咒骂天气太热，捂着头
思索命运和未来
再等一天可就太晚了

"去拿我的外套和领带
还有钱能买到的最便宜劳力
给黄骠马备鞍
若见我久去不归，就祷告。"

哦，他们骑了一整夜，他们骑了一整日
沿着大路一直向东

His spirit was tired and his vision was bent
His men deserted him and onward he went

He came to a place where the light was dull
His forehead pounding in his skull
Heavy heart was wracked with pain
Insomnia raging in his brain

Well he threw down his helmet and his cross-handled sword
He renounced his faith, he denied his Lord
Crawled on his belly, put his ear to the wall
One way or another he'd put an end to it all

He leaned down, cut the electric wire
Stared into the flames and he snorted the fire
Peered through the darkness, caught a glimpse of the two
It was hard to tell for certain who was who

He lowered himself down on a golden chain
His nerves were quaking in every vein
His knuckles were bloody, he sucked in the air
He ran his fingers through his greasy hair

They looked at each other and their glasses clinked
One single unit inseparably linked
"Got a strange premonition there's a man close by."

他神思恍恍，视线暗下去
部下舍弃他，而他继续前行

他来到一个灯光昏暗的地方
前额在头骨中咚咚响
沉重的心痛得要裂开了
失眠在脑海中肆虐

哦他扔下头盔和十字柄的剑
宣布放弃信仰，否定了他的上帝
他匍匐前进，将耳朵贴墙
管它怎样他要做个了断

他弯下身，割断电线
眼瞪着赤焰，鼻息里喷出火
望穿黑暗，扫见那两人
难以确定究竟谁是谁

他用金链将自己放下去
每根血管的神经都在哆嗦
指关节血淋淋，他用力吸气
指头从黏腻的头发穿过

那两人对视着，酒杯相碰
连成不可分的整体
"我有种奇怪的预感，有个男人在附近。"

"Don't worry about him, he wouldn't harm a fly."

From behind the curtain the boss crossed the floor
He moved his feet and he bolted the door
Shadows hiding the lines in his face
With all the nobility of an ancient race

She turned, she was startled with a look of surprise
With a hatred that could hit the skies
"You're a reckless fool, I can see it in your eyes.
To come this way was by no means wise."

"Get up, stand up, you greedy lipped wench
And cover your face or suffer the consequence.
You are making my heart full sick.
Put your clothes back on double quick."

"Silly boy, you think me a saint.
I'll listen no more to your words of complaint.
You've given me nothing but the sweetest lies.
Now hold your tongue and feed your eyes."

"I'd have given you the stars and the planets too
But what good would these things do you?
Bow the heart, if not the knee
Or never again this world you'll see."

"别担心他，他连只苍蝇都不会伤害。"

主人从帘后现身，穿过屋子
移动着脚步，拴上了门
阴影藏起他脸上的纹路
连同古老家族的尊贵举止

她转过身，一脸错愕震惊
还有冲天的厌憎
"你这个鲁莽蠢货，从你眼里看得出。
你这么跑来太不明智。"

"起来，站起来，你这个贪嘴荡妇
遮上你的脸，否则后果自负。
你让我恶心。
快把衣服穿回去。"

"傻孩子，你当我是圣女。
我不会再听你的抱怨。
你除了最甜美的谎言，什么都没给我。
住口吧，张开眼睛看看。"

"我本来要给你恒星和行星
但这些东西于你何用？
低头吧，就算不屈膝
否则你再也看不到这个世界。"

"Oh, please let not your heart be cold.
This man is dearer to me than gold."
"Oh my dear, you must be blind.
He's a gutless ape with a worthless mind."

"You had your way too long with me.
Now it's me who'll determine how things shall be.
Try to escape," he cussed and cursed
"You'll have to try to get past me first."

"I dare not let your passion rule.
You think my heart, the heart of a fool.
And you sir, you cannot deny
You made a monkey of me, what and for why?"

"I'll have no more of this insulting chat.
The devil can have you, I'll see to that.
Look sharp or step aside,
Or in the cradle you'll wish you died."

The gun went boom and the shot rang clear
First bullet grazed his ear
Second ball went right straight in
And he bent in the middle like a twisted pin

"啊，请不要这么冷血。
这人于我比金子更贵重。"
"啊我的爱人，你一定是瞎了眼。
他就是个没种的猿猴，他的心不值一文。"

"长久以来都是我由着你。
现在该由我来决断此事。
想跑吗，"他咒骂着
"先过了我这关再说。"

"我不敢奢求你克制冲动。
你想想我的心，这一颗傻瓜的心。
可是你先生，你不能否认
你让我难堪，这是干吗，为什么？"

"我不会再继续这侮辱人的对话。
魔鬼会拥有你，我会看见。
眼睛放亮，或者让过一边儿，
若不想早死的话。"

枪轰然爆响，子弹呼啸
第一颗擦过耳朵
第二颗径直射入
他像根扭曲的别针从中间弯下去

He crawled to the corner and he lowered his head
He gripped the chair and he grabbed the bed
It would take more than needle and thread
Bleeding from the mouth, he's as good as dead

"You shot my husband down, you fiend."
"Husband, what husband, what the hell do you mean?
He was a man of strife, a man of sin.
I cut him down and I'll throw him to the wind."

"Hear this," she said, with angry breath
"You too shall meet the lord of death.
It was I who brought your soul to life."
And she raised her robe and she drew out a knife

His face was hard and caked with sweat
His arms ached and his hands were wet
"You're a murderous queen and a bloody wife.
If you don't mind, I'll have the knife."

"We're two of a kind and our blood runs hot.
But we're no way similar in body and thought.
All husbands are good men, as all wives know."
Then she pierced him to the heart and his blood did flow

His knees went limp and he reached for the door

他爬向屋角，垂下头
握着椅子，抓住了床
针和线已经不管用了
嘴里流出血，他就要死了

"你杀了我丈夫，你这恶魔。"
"丈夫，什么丈夫，你什么意思？
他是个祸根，一个罪人。
我除掉他，把他丢入风中。"

"听着，"她说，怒火填膺，
"你也应该见死神。
是我给你的灵魂以生命。"
说着她掀起睡袍，拔出一把刀

他面部僵硬，沾满了汗
臂膀疼痛，手心全湿了
"你这个凶残女魔头，该死的人妻。
回心转意吧，把刀给我。"

"我们俩是同类，血都很热。
但身体和思想没一点相像。
所有丈夫都是好人，所有妻子都知道。"
然后她刺穿了他的心，鲜血流淌

他膝盖软下去，他伸手去抓门

His doom was sealed, he slid to the floor
He whispered in her ear, "This is all your fault.
My fighting days have come to a halt."

She touched his lip and kissed his cheek
He tried to speak, but his breath was weak
"You died for me, now I'll die for you."
She put the blade to her heart and she ran it through

All three lovers together in a heap
Thrown into the grave forever to sleep
Funeral torches blazed away
Through the towns and the villages all night and all day

他在劫难逃，他跌倒在地
他在她耳边低声说："都是你的错，
我的战斗生涯就此完结。"

她触他的唇，吻他的脸
他想说话，却已气息奄奄
"你为我而死，现在我也为你死。"
她举刀刺向自己的心，一刀刺穿

三个恋人堆成一堆
扔进了坟墓永远沉睡
葬礼的火把火光飞逝
穿过城镇和村庄，整夜又整日

TEMPEST

The pale moon rose in its glory
Out on the western town
She told a sad, sad story
Of the great ship that went down

'Twas the fourteen day of April
Over the waves she rode
Sailing into tomorrow
To a golden age foretold

The night was bright with starlight
The seas were sharp and clear
Moving through the shadows
The promised hour was near

Lights were holding steady
Gliding over the foam
All the lords and ladies
Heading for their eternal home

The chandeliers were swaying
From the balustrades above

暴风雨

寒月自辉光中升起
在西部小镇上空
她讲述着悲伤、悲伤的故事
关于那艘沉没巨轮

那是四月第十四日
她行驶在浪涛间
驶入明天
驶向预言中的黄金岁月

那一晚星光映夜色
大海轮廓鲜明而清澈
穿过阴影移动
允诺的时辰近了

灯光始终平稳
滑过泡沫
各位王公贵妇
前往他们永恒的家

枝形吊灯摇晃
在楼梯栏杆上面

The orchestra was playing
Songs of faded love

The watchman he lay dreaming
As the ballroom dancers twirled
He dreamed the Titanic was sinking
Into the underworld

Leo took his sketchbook
He was often so inclined
He closed his eyes and painted
The scenery in his mind

Cupid struck his bosom
And broke it with a snap
The closest woman to him
He fell into her lap

He heard a loud commotion
Something sounded wrong
His inner spirit was saying
That he couldn't stand here long

He staggered to the quarterdeck
No time now to sleep
Water on the quarterdeck

管弦乐队演奏着
凋谢的爱情之歌

守夜人躺着在做梦
当舞厅里舞者旋转
他梦到泰坦尼克号下沉
沉入那冥界阴间

利奥拿起素描本
他时常有这种冲动
他闭上眼睛描画
存在于脑海的风景

丘比特射中他的心
一声轻响，透胸而入
与他最近的女人
他倒进了她的怀中

他听见一片喧腾
像是出了什么事
他心里有声音说
不能再待下去

他蹒跚着摸向后甲板
再没时间睡觉了
后甲板的水

Already three foot deep

Smokestack leaning sideways
Heavy feet began to pound
He walked into the whirlwind
Sky spinning all around

The ship was going under
The universe opened wide
The roll was called up yonder
The angels turned aside

Lights down in the hallway
Flickering dim and dull
Dead bodies already floating
In the double bottomed hull

The engines then exploded
Propellers they failed to start
The boilers overloaded
The ship's bow split apart

Passengers were flying
Backward, forward, far and fast
They mumbled, fumbled, tumbled
Each one more weary than the last

已经有三尺高了

烟囱歪向一边
咚咚咚脚步沉重
他走进一片混乱
四周天空旋转

船在往下沉
宇宙张大口
那边在点名
天使别过头

走廊里的灯
昏暗不明闪烁
尸体已浮上来
在双层底的船中

随后引擎爆炸
螺旋桨无法启动
锅炉过载
船头裂开

乘客在飞
向后、向前，又快又远
他们嘟哝，摸索，翻滚
一个比一个疲倦

The veil was torn asunder
'Tween the hours of twelve and one
No change, no sudden wonder
Could undo what had been done

The watchman lay there dreaming
At forty-five degrees
He dreamed the Titanic was sinking
Dropping to her knees

Wellington, he was sleeping
His bed began to slide
His valiant heart was beating
He pushed the tables aside

Glass of shattered crystal
Lay scattered 'round about
He strapped on both his pistols
How long could he hold out?

His men and his companions
Were nowhere to be seen
In silence there he waited for
Time and space to intervene

面纱撕破
在十二点到一点间
无改变，无奇迹
将已发生的事回转

守夜人躺在那儿做梦
呈四十五度
他梦到泰坦尼克号下沉
落向她的双膝

惠灵顿在酣眠
床开始滑
勇士的心跳动
他将桌子推向一边

玻璃像碎水晶
碎落四周
他绑紧双枪
他能抵挡多久？

手下和同伴
四望已不见
寂静中他等待
时间空间出面

The passageway was narrow
There was blackness in the air
He saw every kind of sorrow
Heard voices everywhere

Alarm bells were ringing
To hold back the swelling tide
Friends and lovers clinging
To each other side by side

Mothers and their daughters
Descending down the stairs
Jumped into the icy waters
Love and pity sent their prayers

The rich man, Mr. Astor
Kissed his darling wife
He had no way of knowing
Be the last trip of his life

Calvin, Blake and Wilson
Gambled in the dark
Not one of them would ever live to
Tell the tale of disembark

Brother rose up against brother

走道狭窄
空气黑沉沉
他看到各种惨剧
听到四处人声

警报声大作
提醒舱内积水上升
友人恋人依偎着
肩并肩人挨人

母亲们女儿们
往楼梯下面爬
她们跳进冰冷的海水
爱和怜悯送出她们的祷告

富翁埃斯特先生
吻他的爱妻
他无从知晓
这是他人生最后的行旅

卡尔文、布莱克和威尔逊
在黑暗中打赌
赌他们没一个会活下来
给人讲上岸故事

兄弟同室操戈

In every circumstance
They fought and slaughtered each other
In a deadly dance

They lowered down the lifeboats
From the sinking wreck
There were traitors, there were turncoats
Broken backs and broken necks

The bishop left his cabin
To help all those in need
Turned his eyes up to the heavens
Said, "The poor are yours to feed."

Davey the brothel keeper
Came out, dismissed his girls
Saw the water getting deeper
Saw the changing of his world

Jim Dandy smiled
He'd never learned to swim
Saw the little crippled child
And he gave his seat to him

He saw the starlight shining
Streaming from the East

情形各式各样
他们自相残杀
跳着死亡之舞

他们从沉船的残骸
放下救生艇
有背叛者，有变节者
折断的腰和摔折的颈

主教离开舱房
帮助所有需要帮助的
他抬眼望着穹苍
说："这些可怜人归您供养。"

妓院班头戴维
出来遣散姑娘们
他看见水越来越深
看见他的世界正在改变

吉姆·丹迪笑了
他没学过游泳
他看到跛脚孩童
将位子让给他

他看到星光闪亮
从东方喷涌

Death was on the rampage
But his heart was now at peace

They battened down the hatches
But the hatches wouldn't hold
They drowned upon the staircase
Of brass and polished gold

Leo said to Cleo
"I think I'm going mad."
But he'd lost his mind already
Whatever mind he had

He tried to block the doorway
To save all those from harm
Blood from an open wound
Pouring down his arm

Petals fell from flowers
'Til all of them were gone
In the long and dreadful hours
The wizard's curse played on

The host was pouring brandy
He was going down slow
He stayed right 'til the end

死亡横冲直撞
但他心中一片安宁

他们用板条封舱
但舱门抵不住
他们溺毙在楼梯上
楼梯上镶铜镀金

利奥对克利奥说
"我觉得我要疯了。"
可他已经疯了
不管他有怎样的心智

他奋力堵住入口
让大家免受灾祸
血从伤口涌出来
顺着胳膊流下

花朵上花瓣纷纷
直到全部落尽
漫长可怕的时间
巫师诅咒还在上演

船主倒着白兰地
缓缓沉下海去
他坚守到终点

He was the last to go

There were many, many others
Nameless here forevermore
They'd never sailed the ocean
Or left their homes before

The watchman, he lay dreaming
The damage had been done
He dreamed the Titanic was sinking
And he tried to tell someone

The captain, barely breathing
Kneeling at the wheel
Above him and beneath him
Fifty thousand tons of steel

He looked over at his compass
And he gazed into its face
Needle pointing downward
He knew he lost the race

In the dark illumination
He remembered bygone years
He read the Book of Revelation
And he filled his cup with tears

他最后一个离船

还有许多许多人
不知姓名永被遗忘
他们从未航过海
以前不曾离开家乡

守夜人躺着在做梦
灾难业已铸成
他梦到泰坦尼克号下沉
他想将消息告诉他人

船长奄奄一息
跪在舵轮旁
在他上面和下面
是五万吨钢

他望向罗盘
瞪着它的盘面
指针指向下
他明白他输了

暗光之中
他想起过去的日子
那天他读《启示录》
泪水注满了杯子

When the Reaper's task had ended
Sixteen hundred had gone to rest
The good, the bad, the rich, the poor
The loveliest and the best

They waited at the landing
And they tried to understand
But there is no understanding
On the judgment of God's hand

News came over the wires
And struck with deadly force
Love had lost its fires
All things had run their course

The watchman he lay dreaming
Of all things that can be
He dreamed the Titanic was sinking
Into the deep blue sea

收割者作业告终
一千六百人归去安歇
好人、坏人、富人、穷人
最可爱的和最优秀的

他们在码头等候
他们试图理解
但上帝手中的判决
是无法理解的

电波传来消息
带来致命打击
爱失去火焰
万事如常继续

守夜人躺着在做梦
梦到可能的一切
他梦到泰坦尼克号下沉
沉入深蓝海底

ROLL ON JOHN

Doctor, doctor, tell me the time of day
Another bottle's empty, another penny spent
He turned around and he slowly walked away
They shot him in the back and down he went

Shine your light
Move it on
You burned so bright
Roll on, John

From the Liverpool docks to the red light Hamburg streets
Down in the quarry with the Quarrymen
Playing to the big crowds, playing to the cheap seats
Another day in the life on your way to your journey's end

Shine your light
Move it on
You burned so bright
Roll on, John

前进约翰

医生，医生，告诉我现在什么时辰
又一瓶酒空了，又一便士花了
他转过身，他缓缓走去
他们从背后射中他，他倒下去

放射你的光
继续向前
你燃烧得如此明亮
前进啊，约翰

从利物浦码头到汉堡红灯区
与"采石工"[2]一起去采石场
为大众演，为便宜座儿演
生命中的又一天，你走你的路，去旅途终点

放射你的光
继续向前
你燃烧得如此明亮
前进啊，约翰

---

[1]　约翰，指约翰·列侬。
[2]　"采石工"，披头士乐队的前身。

Sailing through the trade winds bound for the South

Rags on your back just like any other slave

They tied your hands and they clamped your mouth

Wasn't no way out of that deep, dark cave

Shine your light

Move it on

You burned so bright

Roll on, John

I heard the news today, oh boy

They hauled your ship up on the shore

Now the city gone dark, there is no more joy

They tore the heart right out and cut it to the core

Shine your light

Move it on

You burned so bright

Roll on, John

Put down your bags and get 'em packed

Leave right now, you won't be far from wrong

乘着信风向南行驶
你衣衫褴褛就像其他奴隶
他们捆你的手他们封你的嘴
那又深又黑的洞穴没有出路 [1]

放射你的光
继续向前
你燃烧得如此明亮
前进啊，约翰

今天我听了新闻，噢天
他们把你的船拖上岸
现在城市一片黑，再没有欢乐
他们把那颗心扯出来，从中间剖开

放射你的光
继续向前
你燃烧得如此明亮
前进啊，约翰

放下你的行囊，将它收拾好
现在就离开，断不会错

---

[1] "那又深又黑的洞穴没有出路"，披头士早年在利物浦的"洞穴俱乐
部"演出。

The sooner you go, the quicker you'll be back
You been cooped up on an island far too long

Shine your light
Move it on
You burned so bright
Roll on, John

Slow down, you're moving way too fast
Come together right now over me
Your bones are weary, you're about to breathe your last
Lord, you know how hard that it can be

Shine your light
Move it on
You burned so bright
Roll on, John

Roll on John, roll through the rain and snow
Take the right hand road and go where the buffalo roam
They'll trap you in an ambush 'fore you know
Too late now to sail back home

Shine your light
Move it on
You burned so bright

走得越早，回来便越快
你被困岛上已经太长时间

放射你的光
继续向前
你燃烧得如此明亮
前进啊，约翰

慢一些啊，你走得太快
到我这儿来吧，和我一起
你太累了，快剩最后一口气
主啊，你知道这多么不易

放射你的光
继续向前
你燃烧得如此明亮
前进啊，约翰

前进约翰，穿过雪和雨
走右边道，去野牛漫游地
他们会埋伏诱捕你，趁你茫然无知
现在往家赶为时已迟

放射你的光
继续向前
你燃烧得如此明亮

Roll on, John

Tyger, tyger, burning bright
I pray the Lord my soul to keep
In the forest of the night
Cover him over, and let him sleep

Shine your light
Move it on
You burned so bright
Roll on, John

前进啊，约翰

老虎，老虎，燃烧的火光
求主守护我的灵魂
在黑夜的丛林里
给他盖好啊，让他安息

放射你的光
继续向前
你燃烧得如此明亮
前进啊，约翰